D1624829

Praise for
This Is My Body

"I honestly don't think there is a book out there like this one that is quite so brave and honest about the complex, pain-filled, and beautiful experience so many of us have with our bodies. I applaud Ragan Sutterfield for bringing to the light what has for so long been hiding in the dark."

> —NADIA BOLZ-WEBER, author of *Pastrix: The Cranky, Beautiful Faith of a Sinner and Saint*

"Ragan has learned from experience what our best poets have been telling us—the key to being human in our time is a 'recovered body.' That the 'soft animal of your body' will teach you, like the wild geese, if you give it your attention. What Ragan makes so beautifully clear is how Jesus longs to love and redeem us in and through our bodies. *This Is My Body* is a memoir that threatens to upend spiritual writing in the twenty-first century."

> —JONATHAN WILSON-HARTGROVE, author of *Strangers at My Door: A True Story of Finding Jesus in Unexpected Guests*

"Ragan Sutterfield not only reminds us that we live our faith in our bodies, but he calls us to live with beauty, grace, and strength. *This is My Body* is the ideal companion as we seek to live whole healed lives in mind, body, and spirit."

> —DOUG PAGITT, author of *Flipped: The Provocative Truth That Changes Everything We Know About God*

"'We are practicing for forever.' That's the last sentence of this remarkable book, in which Ironman meets the Jesus Prayer, and every preceding word leads up to it. At a time when so many memoirs seem to be driven by a terminal narcissism, Ragan Sutterfield's story of transformation lifts us out of relentless self-preoccupation."

—JOHN WILSON, editor, *Books & Culture*

"Ragan Sutterfield has intensely lived a struggle in pursuit of fulfillment. In *This Is My Body,* he rehearses this struggle in vivid and engrossing detail, from encroaching obesity to a broken marriage to completing marathons and a grueling triathlon. His story is unflinchingly honest and encouraging for all of us who want to be whole, body and soul."

—RODNEY CLAPP, author of *Tortured Wonders: Christian Spirituality for People, Not Angels*

THIS IS MY BODY

THIS IS MY BODY

From Obesity to Ironman, My Journey
into the True Meaning of Flesh, Spirit, and Deeper Faith

RAGAN SUTTERFIELD

CONVERGENT
BOOKS®

THIS IS MY BODY
PUBLISHED BY CONVERGENT BOOKS

Scripture quotations are taken from the New Revised Standard Version of the Bible, copyright © 1989 by the Division of Christian Education of the National Council of the Churches of Christ in the USA. Used by permission. All rights reserved. Scripture quotations marked (NIV) are taken from the Holy Bible, New International Version®, NIV®. Copyright © 1973, 1978, 1984, 2011 by Biblica Inc.™ Used by permission of Zondervan. All rights reserved worldwide. www.zondervan.com.

Details in some anecdotes and stories have been changed to protect the identities of the persons involved.

Hardcover ISBN 978-1-60142-551-5
eBook ISBN 978-1-60142-553-9

Copyright © 2015 by Ragan Sutterfield

Cover design by Kristopher K. Orr; cover image by Woods Wheatcroft, Corbis Images

Published in association with the literary agency of Wendy Sherman, Wendy Sherman Associates, Inc., 27 W. 24th St., Suite 700B, New York, NY 10010.

All rights reserved. No part of this book may be reproduced or transmitted in any form or by any means, electronic or mechanical, including photocopying and recording, or by any information storage and retrieval system, without permission in writing from the publisher.

Published in the United States by Convergent Books, an imprint of the Crown Publishing Group, a division of Random House LLC, New York, a Penguin Random House Company.

CONVERGENT BOOKS and its open book colophon are registered trademarks of Random House LLC.

Library of Congress Cataloging-in-Publication Data
Sutterfield, Ragan.
    This is my body : from obesity to ironman, my journey into the true meaning of flesh, spirit, and deeper faith / Ragan Sutterfield.—First Edition.
        pages cm
    ISBN 978-1-60142-551-5—ISBN 978-1-60142-553-9 (electronic) 1. Human body—Religious aspects—Christianity. 2. Sutterfield, Ragan. I. Title.
    BT741.3.S88 2015
    233'.5—dc23
                                                            2014035477

Printed in the United States of America
2015—First Edition

10 9 8 7 6 5 4 3 2 1

SPECIAL SALES
Most Convergent books are available at special quantity discounts when purchased in bulk by corporations, organizations, and special-interest groups. Custom imprinting or excerpting can also be done to fit special needs. For information, please e-mail SpecialMarkets@ConvergentBooks.com or call 1-800-603-7051.

For my wife, who loved my body from the start and showed me the way to wholeness.

Contents

Witness

"Can I get a witness?"

This common call of Spirit-filled pastors, so often parodied, is in fact a call to something good and true and necessary. As human beings we can't find truth on our own; we need the experiences of others to help us find our meaning. Those of us who have discovered something good in all the confusion of the world need to testify to the ways in which our lives have found their fullness. This book is my witness, my testimony, of how I finally experienced God not as some disembodied spirit in a faraway heaven, but in the very echo of my flesh.

We live in a time in which we are barraged with a multitude of messages about what our bodies should look like, what purposes they should serve, and what bearing they should have on our minds and spirits. As a result, most of us have assembled troubled images in our heads of what it means to have a "good body." We've been told that a good body is one that produces all the right numbers (blood pressure, cholesterol, body mass index) and has all the right dimensions, though definitions of what's "right" vary depending on whom you ask. We've been sold a standard that's delivered via the grocery store magazine rack. A good body is sexy and it is lean, we're told. It is never weak, disordered, diseased, or broken.

The cacophony of opinions about what our bodies should be is so loud, it's hard to listen for the voices that matter. Many of us are tempted, as I was, to just forget it all and let our bodies give in to one addiction or another. Others of us strive to perfect our bodies, obsessing over every muscle curve and wrinkle of our skin. I've done that too.

Don't be vain.

Don't be a glutton.

It's just a shell.

Religious teachers rarely help us through the mess. Their own messages represent a confusing range of contradictions. Few of them tell us that our bodies are good and glorious. The body for most is a burden, a weight that can drag us down toward a host of sins. A shell we will cast off when we can finally live as spirits in a faraway heaven.

I heard and lived all these messages, but God whispered to me another word. Through love and prayer and running long miles, I discovered something else about my body: it is a gift, a sign of God's love in the world. Yours is too. Whatever your shape and whatever struggles you've had with your body, these facts are true right now, not at some point down the road when heavenly perfection will be achieved.

"Can I get a witness?" the preacher calls.

Here I go.

20 Weeks to Ironman

After midnight
Ouachita National Forest

I'm just past the 26.2-mile marathon mark, and I still have another four and a half miles until the finish. It's around 1:30 a.m., and I've been running for over five hours, up and down the gravel service roads of the Ouachita National Forest in western Arkansas. There's no moon. The sky is overcast. I wish I'd spent more time searching for my good headlamp because the spare I brought is going dim, making only one small circle of light in the darkness. They say that copperhead snakes like to spread out on these roads at night, seeking warmth for their cold blood from the sun-baked rocks and gravel.

"Lord Jesus Christ, son of God, have mercy on me, a sinner." The Jesus Prayer, treasured in the Eastern Orthodox tradition, comes to mind whenever I run long, and now in the dark it takes on special meaning. A nineteenth-century book, *The Way of a Pilgrim,* recounts the journey of a simple Russian monk who learned to internalize this prayer so that it ran continuously in his mind, in the background of every thought. J. D. Salinger set the prayer at the center of his novel *Franny and Zooey,* with Franny proclaiming the prayer to be a way "to see God." Eastern Orthodox monks pray it in the rhythm of their breath, inhaling "Lord Jesus Christ, son of God" and exhaling "have mercy on me, a sinner." This works better in the Greek and Russian languages, with their shorter sentence constructions, than it does in English. When I run I whisper the prayer with my breath. "Lord Jesus Christ" I inhale; "have mercy" I exhale. Early in this Ouachita Forest run my mind raced through random thoughts; I prayed for the people in my life; I watched the sunset. But now I am in complete darkness, alone, with music on my headphones and prayers for mercy on my lips.

This is not my first 50K trail run. I ran one earlier in the year in the Ozark Mountains. That run was difficult to be sure, up and down steep mountains on mostly single-track trails. But there I ran in daylight, and I could see other runners all around. It was a beautiful place, full of mountain wonder. Now I am by myself. I see a headlight bobbing here and there, ahead and behind me, but I feel alone. I'm reminded of the times I've been in caves, unable to tell whether it's day or night, my senses deprived by the darkness.

Yet I also feel a kind of purity. The everyday world is gone, and I am somehow suspended in a space that is both physically raw and spiritual. Every breath and every thought in my being seems present in each effort to move a foot forward. I have to bring everything to the work of moving my body, and with the conscious contraction of each muscle, it is as though my whole self suddenly becomes clear to me as I push toward the finish. I am neither body nor mind; I am simply "I" in my entirety. They say Plato was a runner, but I doubt he went for distance. If he had, he could have never thought the soul and body separate.

My legs are past tired, but it doesn't matter. There's a phrase ultrarunners use to get them past the marathon mark, past the point at which a run becomes an "ultra." "Perpetual forward motion," they say to move toward those final miles. Sprinters don't say it; neither do runners of 5Ks or 10Ks. These runners never get to the kind of exhausted crisis that calls for this mantra. "Perpetual forward motion" comes to mind around the twenty-six-mile point on longer distance runs, like this ultramarathon, for even the most accomplished runners.

"Perpetual forward motion" is a principle that distinguishes endurance sports from every other work of athleticism. There is tremendous focus in weightlifting, in which the body, mind, and soul come into alignment. A game of soccer can remind one of the power of the flesh. Baseball can call the body into great precision, and throwing and catching the irrationally oblong football requires an incredible integration of physical and mental quickness. But it is only in endurance sports, such as distance running, marathon swimming, the Ironman triathlon, and Nordic skiing, that the body is called into a continuous exertion that requires one to completely let go and release everything to forward motion, or else lie down on the side of the road and wait for the sag-wagon truck to come pick up the athletes who can't make it to the course's end.

In this Arkansas night, "perpetual forward motion" comes to me just after the last aid station—an oasis of light in the formless void of night. The station stands just before the last seven-mile stretch, floodlights in the woods illuminating tables stacked with peanut-butter-and-jelly sandwiches, pickles, pretzels, gummy bears, Gatorade, soda, and water. It's strange what I want to eat after running for five hours. I cram down pretzels and half a PB & J, wash them down with flat Mountain Dew, and start back on the road. A few yards down I come across another runner who is bent over, throwing up—a casualty to the tricky challenge of eating enough to stay fueled on the trail but not so much that the stomach rebels.

After the aid station there is just darkness and my personal circle of light. *Perpetual forward motion.* I keep my eyes out for glow sticks tied to trees and bushes, the markers for the right road. I spot one up ahead, just as I see another runner heading off in the wrong direction. I yell and watch his headlamp turn as he corrects his route. That would have been bad. That could have been me. *Perpetual forward motion.* "Lord Jesus Christ, have mercy on me, a sinner," I pray as Nirvana's "Scentless Apprentice" blares through my headphones.

With only 5K left to go, I start to pass runners who are now walking. I want to stop with them; my pace is now barely a run. We've gone twenty-eight miles, yet it's here that I want to stop, the flow of my legs giving way to an unbearable heaviness. I suddenly realize that it's almost 2 a.m. and I usually go to sleep at 9 p.m. *Why am I in the woods? Why am I doing this?* A woman twice my age wearing a big pink visor runs up beside me. "I've run over twenty of these," she calls. "You just have to keep running." *Perpetual forward motion.*

Just around a bend in the road we come upon another runner. I recognize him as a guy who humiliated me at my local running club's sprint workout a few weeks earlier. Back then, he lapped me on the track as I ran 800m repeats. Now he sits on the side of a dirt road with his head in his hands.

The woman with the visor stops. "Come on," she says. "You've got to keep going."

"I just need a minute." He waves us away.

I look at my Garmin GPS watch. *Two miles to go.* I lean my body forward and focus all my remaining will, every atom of energy I can summon in my body, on lifting my feet off the ground. It's time for gravity to do its work; my legs just have to catch my fall. Lift, fall, catch…lift, fall, catch. *Perpetual forward motion.*

At half a mile to go, we hit the pavement that leads into the forest service recreation area where the finish line awaits. I pick up the pace; I give everything I have to the effort of reaching that light up ahead. *Forward motion, forward motion, forward motion.* Other runners are gathered, cheering us on as we stumble in. I run with all the remaining strength I can muster. There are volunteers at the finish line to catch us as we stop, if needed, and many runners do collapse when the forward motion finally ceases. My legs feel wobbly, but I manage to limp over to a bench. My head is spinning. I reach down to my shoes and realize they are full of sweat—little puddles in the bottom soaking into the insoles. I stare at the post-race food table, and I am suddenly hungry in a fierce way. I manage to stagger to the line, quickly devour a hot dog, and gulp down Coke.

My body has been to the edge of its possibility. I hurt, I am exhausted, but I also feel like my body has begun to tap into a purpose and reality I could never find in an office chair or even in a jog around the block. My legs are chafed and heavy with lactic acid; my muscles cramping, I climb into the back of a friend's car for the ride home.

In a few months I'll begin a similar endurance race, but at that race I'll have swum 2.4 miles and biked 112 miles before even starting the marathon. In a few months I'll attempt to be more than an ultrarunner who can run more than thirty-one miles in one stretch.

I'll try to become an Ironman.

This Is My Young Body

When I was growing up, I was a kid who lived in the woods and in my head. It would be inaccurate to say I wasn't physically active, because I hiked through the forest with my friends along dry creek beds, searching among the rocks for Indian artifacts. I climbed trees—big sweet gums by a nearby lake—and built tree houses that overlooked beaver dams. I loved to explore, to walk and run, to follow animal trails wherever they led. But when it came to sports, the venue through which American culture primarily acknowledges and celebrates the bodies of boys, I always felt like a failure. I tried every sport I could: basketball, baseball, football. I didn't excel at any of them.

I did get credit for other achievements. "Wow, you have such a big vocabulary!" adults said. Or, "You really know a lot for a ten-year-old." Those positive reinforcements drove me to try to fulfill their expectations of my mind through afternoons spent reading books or conducting haphazard science experiments. But when it came to my body and to my use of it, people were mostly silent.

The one partial exception was swimming, a sport in which I showed ability in form, though not in speed. There are no trophies for an excellent swim stroke, no awards for perfect form. It doesn't matter if you can run beautifully or swim beautifully; it matters only whether you're fast. "You have a beautiful stroke," I was often told, but I never won a meet or even a heat—events that filled me with a mix of chlorine headache and anxiety, and left me feeling slow and out of breath. I was so burned out on swimming by junior high that I didn't swim laps in a pool again until I was in my twenties. So it happened that I grew up seeing myself as a "brain," playing to what I saw as my strengths. My body became for me something to get out of the way so that my mind could show through.

Besides being a "brain" with a mind, I was also a "church kid" with a spirit. I attended Sunday and Wednesday youth group every week, from sixth grade until I left home for college. At that time, my family went to a suburban megachurch that was co-led by a former college football star. Whenever the Arkansas Razorbacks or Dallas Cowboys were scheduled to play in the afternoon, we could count on the promise that the worship of God would end by game time. The kids in the youth group weren't just influenced by this sports-obsessed culture; they were shaped by it. It seemed like every girl wanted to be with a "jock" and every boy was fluent in football. The dominant men's fashion was a polo shirt paired with a white University of Arkansas baseball cap.

This was a preppy, affluent place. But it wasn't my place. I became a skateboarder partly for the joy of the board, but more so to be a cultural skater. I was never any good at the actual skateboarding part, unable to move past the basic "Ollie" jump. The kickflip I always practiced required a coordination my body seemed to lack, the board always landing with its wheels in the air and me, on the ground. But among the skateboarders that didn't seem to matter. Skateboarding was a way for us to embrace a cool that was different from that of the jocks who sat at the top of the social ladder of our megachurch youth group.

It was not only the body in sports but the body in the right kind of clothes that mattered. Junior high is a cruel time, and I had the added disadvantage of being a homeschooled kid in a wealthy church where 80 percent of the kids went to the same prep school. My parents were in nonprofit ministry work, and in an increasingly consumerist culture where expensive brands were becoming dominant, I was out of style. "Salvation is in Jesus," our pastors taught in church. But in the culture of the youth group, salvation was, in reality, a Starter jacket.

A suede jacket or a Starter jacket: those were the two options for the cool kids in early nineties Little Rock, Arkansas. Suede was the preppy choice—a perfect complement for Polo or American Eagle fashions. A Starter jacket was the edgier choice, worn by rappers and skateboarders and jocks alike. Rumor had it you could get beaten up by a gang just for wearing one (a rumor that just added to the appeal). Starter jackets were big and bulky, able to engulf the body I wanted to forget and hide the butt I despised beneath the swirl of their cool. This, I believed, was what would give me a swagger when I walked through the white-hats whose taunts I feared.

I still remember the long conversations with my parents. Suede or Starter: both were upwards of a hundred dollars. That was a lot for a family on a nonprofit salary to spend on a jacket. But my parents saw my sadness and somehow they got the money. We went to the mall and I chose a Raiders Starter jacket: black and white, dark and cool. I couldn't name a single Raiders player; I couldn't care less for the NFL—but I had the symbol, the brand behind which my body could hide. The jacket didn't save me, of course, but for that winter it covered me. I could pull it around me, put up the hood, and feel the vulnerable body beneath disappear.

The theology taught in my youth group didn't really tell us to despise the body; it urged us to forget it. We learned that the body holds dangers and temptations like sex, anorexia, and pride. But the body was not presented as being a part of faith itself. It was a skin we would shed when we shed this earth.

We were not taught that humanity was connected, in creation and salvation, to the humus from which we were formed: Adam from *adamah*—rich, life-giving soil, in the Hebrew. Instead, the vision of salvation we were given was of the disembodied spirit, bodies no longer tied to the earth that God created and called "good." Theological discussions in our church mostly centered around when, exactly, the earth would be destroyed. After "the saved" went to heaven? Or in a slow-burn Tribulation, through which the church would smoke out the unfaithful who couldn't resist the barcodes the Beast would stamp on everyone's foreheads? Our souls were what needed saving; bodies themselves were beyond redemption, like everything else in this world. God had no plans for them, other than for God's children to keep their bodies from sin until we could be saved from our flesh.

Though there was to be no redemption for the body, there existed the possibility of damnation by it. The sins of the body held a special place in the imagination of my megachurch and not just in youth group. Our pastors delivered message after message detailing various bodily dangers as we sat passive in our movie-theater stadium seats. Sex was deemed particularly dangerous: bodily pleasure that could derail a life. I can remember countless sermons and youth talks warning about everything from homosexuality to self-pleasure. But I can't remember hearing a single sermon about greed, caring for the poor, or welcoming the outcasts: subjects at the center of Jesus's teachings.

In this way we missed the central ministry of Jesus, which was a ministry to bodies: healing eyes and legs, raising whole bodies from the dead, feeding thousands of hungry stomachs, turning the water of purity into the wine of celebration at a wedding banquet. But for Jesus-followers in the church of my youth, this concern for flesh and blood was missed. The body was neither a thing of joy nor an object of salvation. It was a dangerous skin that would one day give way to an immaterial spirit—a thing without flesh, without hunger, without sweat.

This theology was often played out at youth rallies in salvation scenarios with two possible endings to our earthly life: death or rapture. We watched evangelistic B-movies about teens who were enjoying the pleasures of life when—*wham!*—a car crash would halt the joy ride. A serious question would be posed: If you died tonight, where would you go? Heaven or hell?

A similar scenario was frequently played out concerning the rapture. One movie featured scenes of cars crashing as Christians suddenly disappeared from the earth. Whether the issue portrayed was rapture or death, the idea was that this life is primarily about not getting into trouble, so that we can get to another life, in another place, where we will exchange our old bodies for new bodies that will be more spirit than flesh.

This line of thinking is a rejection of the creation that God called "good," the creation that Christ entered into to redeem. It communicates explicitly or implicitly that Jesus didn't come to save this world or these bodies. It paints Jesus as a hero who came to evacuate us from a ship that's going down, rather than as a divine repairman who has come to fix the leak. It is a theology that says that this world and these bodies will be left behind.

Such theology has consequences. A church where the soul alone and not the body is saved becomes a place where the body is left to other stories or no story at all. Because the body doesn't matter to our eternal salvation in this view, Christians tend to adopt secular views of the body or simply ignore it and its health altogether. Research has borne this out. According to a Northwestern University study[1] that tracked over two thousand participants for eighteen years, adults like me, who attended evangelical churches as youth, are 50 percent more likely to be obese than our unchurched counterparts. Other research based on census data has shown that Southern Baptists and other, more evangelical denominations are the heaviest of all religious groups. Researchers believe that this could be explained by the low view of the body held in these denominations. If we are all getting new bodies and a new earth, why worry about this body or world?

That standard meal of the church gathering, coffee and doughnuts, is catching up with us. Even more so is our denial of our bodies as objects of God's love and salvation. But what if God is going to save our bodies—these bodies we have now? What if God glories in our flesh? What if God himself became flesh and remains enfleshed? What if God not only has a heart that longs for our love but also a heart that pounds with blood? What if God has skin that drips with sweat? What if the God who offered his body as a sign of love also wants us to experience our bodies as a gift of his love? Christians must worship a God who is all of these things because we worship a God who was made manifest to us in the human, embodied life of Jesus. The denial of the body, of the flesh, is not a denial of the dangerous locus of sin, as so many of us have been taught. It is a denial of the Word made flesh. Those of us who follow Jesus Christ—God in human skin and muscle and mind—cannot deny the goodness of the body. To do so is to reject the reality in which Christ now lives as the risen and ascended Lord.

It was in high school that I first realized I was fat. I had shown a propensity toward heaviness before. But in high school I began to gain weight more noticeably, and people started commenting on it.

When I was in tenth grade, my family moved from Little Rock to a small town in the country. Most of the kids in the local public school had grown up together. They all had stories going back to second grade of the "You remember when Jolene put melted chocolate on Jessica Thompson's chair and said she'd pooped" kind. Coming in as an outsider wasn't easy. Then I met Amber.

Amber was a rough girl from the wrong side of rural culture: not the idyllic farmhouse and forty acres, but the welfare check and trailer. Amber was loud and frank in a way that had been trained out of southern women of the more genteel type. She had freckles, straight brown hair, and was pretty, but seemed unconcerned with her appearance, one way or another.

During my first week of school, lunch was—as it is for new kids and outcasts everywhere—the most troublesome experience. It was during those early weeks that Amber waved me over to her group of friends and said, "Come eat with us." And so I did.

Months later, we were sitting on the concrete courtyard outside of the cafeteria on one of the warmer first days of spring, when Amber commented on my body. I was wearing a T-shirt I liked that had become a bit too small over the winter.

"You have boobs bigger than I do," Amber observed. I smiled and laughed. And stopped wearing T-shirts. She hadn't intended to be mean. She was just frank in a way that people of many cultures are frank. Friends of mine who have worked in Asia and Africa report that it is commonplace for people in many countries to say, "You're getting fat." It's a simple thing to notice, like, "Oh, you changed your hair style." Amber's statement hurt me. Yet there's an element of health to this kind of candor; there's something good about being able to see bodies as honest realities rather than as obsessively watched mirrors that reflect people's worth.

The working classes, those who haven't been fed a lifelong diet of being hailed as the best and the brightest, are often more at ease with the body in all its various forms. Social critic Christopher Lasch wrote in his commentary on contemporary American life, *The Revolt of the Elites:* "While young professionals subject themselves to an arduous schedule of physical exercise and dietary controls designed to keep death at bay…ordinary people, on the other hand, accept the body's decay as something against which it is more or less useless to struggle."[2]

Amber had been speaking from this position of acceptance. But I didn't hear her from that place. I had been raised in the privileged culture of self-making that required perfection of both body and mind. To be fat was unacceptable because being fat would keep me from my ambitions.

Those ambitions in tenth grade centered mostly on winning the affections of a girl—namely Julia, the on-again, off-again girlfriend of our high school's quarterback. Julia had blue eyes and read classic literature on a swing in her father's cow pasture; she took Advanced Placement classes and was captain of the cheerleaders. She was also a ready flirt—a girl with many admirers she did little to discourage. I became one of them. It was Julia I thought of as I walked past food while my stomach burned. It was Julia I thought of when I put on my shoes that spring and started running.

———

Running is the go-to exercise of Americans. It is considered nearly synonymous with "fitness." If you want to "get fit," "lose weight," "look better," or "feel great," running is the ticket, and that's exactly how it's sold, with those two-word promises leaping out from the covers of magazines like *Runner's World.* Running is attractive because, the thinking goes, it takes no training and requires nothing more than shoes. Just lace up.

The reality of running, particularly for beginners, is rather different: bodies unaccustomed to movement, feet and legs broken by thick-soled shoes that force the heel to strike the ground first rather than supporting the way humans naturally run without shoes—landing on the front of the foot. The runners push through the pain, their sagging stomachs sloshing against wet T-shirts. When I run through parks, following popular running paths, I see people trying to get fit for the first time. Their running looks like a painful act—a sadistic contortion down the sidewalk. My first runs were no different. I would lace up and go and see how long I could keep the pain at bay. It seemed to me that the key to successful running was having a high pain tolerance.

"No pain, no gain" has long been the American mantra of exercise. Since we have reduced the pleasures of the body to food and sex, everything else becomes work of the east-of-Eden, post-Fall sort—the "blood, sweat, and tears" kind. We think that to be fit we must go through some kind of mild torture, that this is the price to pay for having a perfect body in a fallen world. It's an attitude toward exercise that hit its stride right around the time obesity rates began their drastic climb in the late 1970s and early 1980s. We can thank Jane Fonda for popularizing the "no pain, no gain" motto.

In the 1980s, Jane Fonda became one in a long series of fitness gurus, from Jack LaLanne to Richard Simmons, who would attempt to lead Americans back to health through exercise. In Jane's case, it was aerobics. In 1982, Fonda produced her first in a series of aerobics videos that were so memorable and representative of the style of the eighties that they're still mocked on *Saturday Night Live*. Wearing leg warmers and bearing light weights, Fonda repeatedly encouraged her viewers with the phrases "Feel the burn" and "No pain, no gain." Pain, we were already pretty sure, was the hallmark of a good workout. Jane Fonda gave us our mantra.

My first runs were certainly painful: clunky jogs down the pavement, trying to beat my body into an object worthy of affection. I had no idea then that running is a skill as technical as swimming. That it takes drills and practice and time to learn to run well. Once those skills are developed, running can be a joy—a movement every bit as natural as walking. There's effort involved, of course, and sweat and deep breaths. But that isn't pain; it's the work of the body, and such work has a pleasure all its own. My first runs, though, were pain filled, and at some point the body insists: No more. Pain is the body's way of saying no, and eventually it makes sure we listen.

Like most beginning runners, I accepted my fate as a moral and physical failure and gave up. I decided I would have to find some other path toward the thinness that would win me Julia's love. If exercise wouldn't get me to my new body, then I'd have to eat my way to perfection. Or better yet, not eat.

———

My efforts toward running and dieting and getting healthy weren't entirely about a girl. There was also a deeper personal side for me: a kind of moral calculus of weight loss. I wanted not just to become thinner but also to be disciplined, to achieve self-mastery. I was motivated by fear. I didn't want to be lazy or morally weak and that was what being fat meant to me. To be fat was to be lacking some essential willpower. I believed that to be an obese person was to be as much of an addict as any gutter alcoholic. I couldn't let that be me.

I had once thought of joining the military because I liked the idea of the discipline. I'd wanted to spit-shine my boots so my reflection showed back. After a good, long period of being a slob, in my junior year of high school I started making my bed daily to military specifications: tight sheets and sharp corners. I had liked the sense of control that discipline gave me. Now, with the death of my career as a runner, I again felt the need to reestablish the power of *my* will.

I'd long had a sense that to be fat represented a moral deficiency. My parents were not overweight, and no one in my family suffered from morbid obesity. My mother, from whom I get my sense of discipline, started exercising when I was in middle school and has been disciplined in exercise and diet for most of my life. But it was not from my family that I picked up this idea of "the immoral obese" that would grow like a monster in my mind. Rather, it was an idea I assembled through accumulation of comments heard here and there, those subtle social cues that young people use as much as anything else to form their moral vision.

The summer before ninth grade I traveled with a youth program to Australia to learn about zoology and marine biology. For nearly a month, we traveled all the way up the coast from Kangaroo Island to Magnetic Island, where we snorkeled on the Great Barrier Reef. While I spent plenty of time with the other students, I was also keen to learn from the adults, most of whom were teachers. One university professor led a walk to the beach every morning, where I witnessed some of the most spectacular sunrises I've ever seen—deep crimson over a black ocean. She also arranged frequent field trips into the bush, where we watched wallabies and tried to spot koalas.

One day, on a field trip to see some of Kangaroo Island's rare orchids, she and I inexplicably got on to the subject of obesity.

"I'm sorry, but I don't like fat people," this professor admitted. "They lack discipline and self-control. They're lazy." The conversation meandered on to other subjects, but in that moment she had named a widely accepted prejudice that had been creeping up in my own consciousness. Though I wasn't what I would become in tenth grade, throughout my childhood I had been just a little pudgy, always a little hesitant to take off my T-shirt in front of anyone. I realized that "fat and happy" was no combination I could ever embody, that fat was no state I could accept.

In high school that prejudice remained, and when I realized I was fat that hatred turned inward, I despised myself. I seized upon discipline and self-control as my answers. I had to overcome. Given that I lacked the athleticism even to run, my path to overcoming would have to be through food. I would discipline my way to a better body. I would starve my way to thinness. I chose as my guides Henry David Thoreau and a big-haired, blond preacher who proclaimed that fat was a sin as bad as any.

When I read *Walden* on a teacher's recommendation, I was drawn to Henry David Thoreau's vision of a simpler life, lived in concert with nature. He wrote: "I believe that water is the only drink for a wise man; wine is not so noble a liquor; and think of dashing the hopes of a morning with a cup of warm coffee, or of an evening with a dish of tea!"[3] Water: pure water. What simpler way could there be to clear the body and mind? I vowed never again to pick up a soda can or coffee cup. I would be like Thoreau and drink nothing but water. I stuck to that vow for that entire summer and most of the rest of high school. That meant I cut out a huge amount of sugar from what had been a regular, high-fructose-corn-syrup Coke habit.

Next came the Weigh Down Workshop, an evangelically based weight-loss program that worked from a kind of Exodus liberation theology to free God's people from fat. My mother read the book during her own journey to health. Later, she summarized it for me and gave me some cassette tapes recorded by the workshop's guru, a woman my mom referred to fondly as "Gwen."

Gwen Shamblin is pastor of a megachurch in Brentwood, Tennessee, a wealthy suburb of Nashville. Her church is organized around the sin of overeating and an apocalyptic worldview that sees her brand of anti-Trinitarian, unorthodox Christianity as the only true way to salvation. In her teachings on diet, Shamblin explains that people who are overweight are enslaved to food, driven just like any addict. And just like Moses's call to the people enslaved in Egypt, God's message to the overweight is this: "Set my people free."

This freedom comes not through the condemnation of any food. Shamblin says that every food from doughnuts to Snickers bars represents some of the goodness God created, even the artificial sweetener aspartame (though other artificial sweeteners are strangely forbidden for being man made). Freedom comes not from resisting a particular kind of food, but from the choice to stop eating when full. Eat only when hungry and stop as soon as you are satisfied. This is the Weigh Down Workshop's commonsense advice.

The Weigh Down Workshop offered me my first clue that there might be something spiritual about how and what we eat. It provided a philosophy of eating, some of it good, but mostly tied up with a moralism around weight that would prove dangerous to me.

Shamblin's teachings were easy to follow and fed into my ambitions of discipline. As I headed into the summer before my junior year, I committed myself fully to my goals. Simplicity, discipline, desire: these were the drivers that led me into my first bout of radical weight loss. If hunger meant a sense of burning, I would wait to eat until I felt a fire. If satiation meant stopping when I felt full, I would take it one step further and stop just before. If any food was permissible, I would eat a carrot but wouldn't touch a doughnut. That summer was all about control, about losing all the weight I could without moderation. I had never been one for grace.

It's five in the morning, and I am on my way to a high-school track. It's been nearly two decades since my graduation. The track is lit with both floodlights and the rising sun.

Click, step, click, step. I warm up with a metronome, counting my footsteps in a 180-beat-per-minute cadence. Then it's 800 meters: two loops around the track as fast as I can sustain. I run until my heart feels strained, my breath sharp inside my chest, my blood crying for oxygen. I walk a quarter of the track in order to rest, then do it all again, five more times. At the end I am spent. I couldn't run another lap, yet it isn't pain that I feel.

To get up day after day and train for the Ironman takes discipline; it requires that same sense of control that drove me to starve myself back in high school. When I finish my run this morning, I'm sweating so much I have to lay out a towel on the car seat to keep the fabric from getting soaked. But unlike on those long-ago days driven by duty and desire, the expression on my face now isn't a grimace. It's a smile. I feel alive in a raw, almost animal-like way. I'm reminded of the point in the movie *Chariots of Fire* when Olympic runner Eric Liddell proclaims, "God made me fast. And when I run, I feel his pleasure." I'm not that fast.

But I feel that pleasure.

Ironman Warm-Up Race

Midmorning
Tunica, Mississippi

I'm running down a Mississippi levee and though it's well before noon, the day is hot with that southern kind of steam that would make a man sweat even while sitting on the porch. The only shade to be found in the whole 6.2-mile run is beneath this little bridge, about two miles in. Some runners are standing under it trying to get a break, exhausted not just by the run but from the hard twenty-five miles we already biked. But I can't stop. There's this guy, another local triathlete I've been talking trash with on Facebook, and I just passed him.

I look down at my GPS sports watch — the holy Garmin — its face reporting my pace, time, distance, heart rate. My heart rate is high: Zone 4 out of 5. I'm going anaerobic, which means my heart is pumping faster than it should to efficiently supply oxygen from my lungs to my muscles. If this were a longer race that would mean the end, my muscles filling with lactic acid, draining the precious stored sugars that provide their energy. But I've been training for this. I can stay at the anaerobic threshold for a while longer, enough to get some distance on my competitors and, hopefully, to make it to the finish line.

This is an out-and-back course, so the athletes ahead of me are running past on the other side of the road, heading in the opposite direction. I see some from my training group, faster guys I wouldn't dream of catching. We exchange high-fives and words of encouragement as we pass each other. That's how it goes in a triathlon—most people are encouraging out on the course because it doesn't matter what anyone else does. At the end of the day, you've run your own race. Still, friendly competition isn't bad either, and there is always someone running about the same pace to push past and to sprint against.

I come through the turnaround and see that I'm almost to the end. Just a few miles to go—a simple 5K to the finish line. Ahead of me runs a man who looks like he's my grandfather's age, and he is clearly in pain. It's an effort of will, his mind forcing his body to go. Above my own breaths, I can hear him gasping for air. If we were any other place I'd be afraid he was about to have a heart attack, but this is an athlete and hard breathing is part of the sport. As I get closer I stare at his calves.

In a triathlon, if you have any competitive instinct whatsoever, you spend a lot of time looking at calves. Most of us shave them: a ritual borrowed from cycling, where hair is seen as an aerodynamic disadvantage and, more importantly, a painful liability when it comes to bandaging the inevitable road rashes caused by bike wrecks.

At the beginning of a race, most organizers will write an athlete's age on the back of her calf with a Sharpie. Unless an athlete is really fast, the best an "age grouper" can hope for is to win first, second, or third in his age division. On the race course, whether on the bike or run, an athlete measures the effort of the person in front of her relative to the number on the back of that person's calf. If I'm coming up behind a cyclist and I know I'm going to have to really push myself to pass him, I weigh whether to exert the effort against his age group. Why bother if he's twenty-five? But if I see a number in the right age group, that's motivation enough to put in the extra effort, to give it all I can.

Coming up behind this old man who's putting forward an effort I can't even imagine making, I spy something more than age marked on his calf. There's an M-dot: the logo of Ironman, a race nearly four times the distance of this one. If you've ever seen a Timex Ironman watch you've seen an M-dot: the figure of a man made of a letter M, with a dot floating above for a head. It's common among triathletes to get a tattoo of the M-dot logo after finishing one's first Ironman. Most get it on the calf, right where other triathletes will see it.

As I pass the man, whose will to finish has already been tested against the even more difficult Ironman, I felt a tremendous sense of respect. And for the first time in my life, I start to wonder about the possibility of getting a tattoo myself. What would that M-dot look like under my age-group number? I wanted what that man had. I wanted to be what that man was.

I wanted to be an Ironman.

⸻

Why would someone want to swim 2.4 miles, bike 112 miles, then run a marathon—all in the same day? It's an absurd act. There are no immediately apparent benefits. Some argue that the Ironman is a goal worth getting in shape for or staying in shape for, but from a fitness perspective there's really nothing healthy about racing that far.

Running and swimming and biking all are great for the body, and there is something fulfilling about these acts that seems to point to humanity's primal roots as endurance athletes, running down antelope in the savannah. So people begin running. They decide they want a challenge and maybe a sticker on their car, so they sign up for a marathon for motivation and as a symbol of health. But what most people don't realize is that after about the half-marathon point, and maybe even before, running gets unhealthy.

If your goal is to lose weight, live a long time, and avoid heart disease, then lift weights, do sprints, go on long walks. Most importantly, eat good food: the kind that comes straight from the earth, especially greens and colorful vegetables, wild fish, and grass-fed meats. These are the kinds of choices that, if practiced with regularity and discipline, can bring people as close to health as their genes and environment will allow.

But racing the 140.6 miles of an Ironman triathlon? Running a marathon? Racing these distances triggers the release of huge amounts of cortisol and adrenaline, the same stress hormones that your body releases when your boss is breathing down your neck or when you get cut off in traffic. In an Ironman or a marathon, good lean muscle is burned for fuel and tremendous stress is placed on the heart, resulting every year in multiple deaths of seemingly fit athletes. If you want to get healthy, lift weights, run a 5K, do some push-ups and pull-ups every other day, but don't run a marathon. By all means don't race an Ironman.

Yet for me, it's right at the 13.1-mile point that things become interesting. Right when the health benefits of the run become dubious. So what is it that makes running for distance so attractive to me and to people like me? Ego could have something to do with it. Tell someone you can run a "sub-twenty-minute 5K," and if they're not a runner they'll say, "Oh, is that good?" Tell someone you can snatch your body weight, and they'll say, "What's a snatch?" Tell someone you competed in an ultramarathon or an Ironman triathlon or rode your bike a hundred miles, and they'll say "Wow!" However, that "Wow" doesn't last long and, unless you really go around bragging, you won't hear that "Wow" very often. It's hardly enough to justify the massive time commitment and relentless work that goes into training for an endurance event. "Wow" isn't the goal; it's icing on the cake.

Why did I want to become an Ironman? Because I wanted to experience even more deeply what I had experienced before in endurance races: a kind of radical presence, a focus and attention unlike anything else, a full integration of myself that was purely here and now but also outside of the normal feeling of time. What I'm describing is something known as "flow."

Flow, this integration of everything in a single moment, is a rare thing. Many people experience something similar when writing, when reading, even when praying. In those moments, time seems to change and everything disappears into the now—no future, no past, just this present moment.

Much of our technological culture works to manufacture a synthetic experience of this flow. Why would a teenage boy sit for five hours playing a video game? Because the passage of time doesn't feel like a waste to him; the hours are meaningless external measures in the face of pure attention and focus. He finds himself entirely absorbed into the game.

But what video games have never given to me, and what I've never experienced in any other way outside of flow, is the full presence of all my parts in the same instant. In flow, no longer do I experience a schizophrenic switching between different facets of myself: *I'm Ragan's brain; I'm Ragan's spirit; I'm Ragan's body.* The only corollary I've found to an endurance event is good sex—open, accepting, full of love. But sex is a different thing: an integration of otherness and self as much as it is a sense of cohesion within the self. Besides, what sex lasts the time it takes to finish an Ironman, around twelve hours on average?

As I started into endurance racing I wanted more and more flow: experiences of my body in concert with my mind, my spirit. Mind and spirit weren't the difficult part. I've always felt able to access them. I've worked as a writer, a teacher, a consultant. I'm a knowledge worker, part of the seemingly high-powered, desirable class of work that much of our education system is geared toward, often at a cost to our physicality. Our society elevates the mind over the body in the workplace, setting the stage for a dualistic approach to our days. Who wants to physically make stuff, to use their bodies, to have sore muscles at the end of the day? Better to have their minds spin over a spreadsheet while their bodies rest in the glow of screens, rising up once in a while to go and eat, or go to the hospital, or to move along on an elliptical, all in the service of keeping the mind going.

And what about the spirit? That ineffable thing, the hard-to-define reality that somehow drives so much of what and who we are? Today, we call it *heart*. The ancient Hebrews called it something like "liver": the very bowels of the self. Though its exact location is hard to place in the body, it is a kind of center to our being—something that seems to be within our bodies but is not entirely the same as our bodies. Science has, of course, tried to sort it out, to explain what we sense in terms of neural networks and brain chemistry. But somehow those explanations are hard to swallow; our language makes it hard to talk in terms of pure material reality. Words such as "love" are resistant to explanation by neurochemistry.

There is a philosophers' joke about philosopher of mind Paul Churchland and neuroscientist Patricia Churchland, who are married. The Churchlands are physicalists who believe that the particulars that make up what we call *mind* or *spirit*, *will* or *heart*, are really functions of the physical stuff of our brains: things that can be explained by the firing of synapses and the release of hormones. So, if love is only a function of a particular cascade of reactions in the brain, how then, goes the joke, do the Churchlands say "I love you"? The answer: "Oh honey, my synapse C35 is really firing right now." The thought of such an explanation for love seems empty; we all feel there's something more happening than chemistry, even those of us who can't accept that this "more" might reveal something of the divine in the world.

Growing up in church, I experienced spirit as something real—a definite part of myself, perhaps more real than anything else about me. My spirit soared to good music. It ached in prayer. I could feel these things. And sometimes my spirit experienced what I later came to recognize as flow, especially in response to something beautiful, often in nature. In college, when I was first experimenting with quiet, contemplative prayer, there were times when it felt as though time began to disappear and my spirit entered a different place, beyond space and time.

But for all of these experiences, my body had never been a part of this flow. It had always been a heavy anchor, dead weight being dragged along. It wasn't until I took up endurance sports—triathlons and ultrarunning—that I experienced in my body what I had experienced in my mind and spirit. It was during the bike portion of my first triathlon that I realized I felt complete at last. My body, my mind, and my soul were all racing down the road together.

Somehow over the distance, my body, too, had entered the picture and had begun to move along not on its own but in concert with everything else. As I swam and biked and ran for distance, I found that my spirit centered my desire to finish, pushing away the questions about quitting that inevitably arise when everything begins to hurt. My brain focused on keeping my legs running in good form and on anticipating my needs (drink water, eat food, etc.), acts that can't be controlled purely by the body because by the time the body knows what it needs, it is often too late.

The late philosopher and teacher Dallas Willard wrote in his beautiful book *Renovation of the Heart* about all the parts that make up the self: the body, the spirit, even our communities. But integrating all of these, bringing them together into a self, he claimed, is what makes up the soul. In an interview in *Perspectives* magazine, Willard described the soul as "the deepest and the most vital part of the person as a whole," saying: "We don't save our soul and leave our emotions and our feelings and our body and all the rest of it out...[The soul] is the thing that integrates all of these aspects of the self and makes them work together."[4] The soul, then, is not only the center of our being but also the thing that brings us coherence—the stitching together of our full selves.

I've always felt my mind and spirit as integrated parts of my self, my soul. But my body has been on the outside, just as my theological upbringing would have wanted it—the body a temporary thing that will disappear at the gates of heaven. I had moved away from this view of the self and salvation, a slow conversion through college and beyond. Through reading writers like Willard and New Testament scholar N. T. Wright, I had begun to learn that such teachings had little to do with what was actually taught in the Bible or in much of Christian tradition. The Gospels in fact go to great lengths to show that Christ resurrected from the dead was not a spirit, but a bodily being. A different kind of body to be sure, able to move without an opening into closed rooms with locked doors. But once there, it was a body that had the scars made by nails and a gaping wound big enough to put a hand into.

When Christ arrived resurrected among the disciples, he didn't come to deliver some esoteric spiritual knowledge that was divorced from the things of this earth; he asked for food and something to drink. This new idea of a bodily resurrection and a bodily ascension into heaven was important because with it offered the hope that our bodies could also be saved. The early father of the church, Gregory of Nyssa, wrote, "What was not assumed was not healed."[5] This meant that whatever Christ didn't take into his nature wasn't a part of the self that would be saved. It would not have made sense for Christ to have only appeared to be human, or to have had a human body but not a human mind. To save us, Christ had to be fully human—in every way that we are human, including our bodies.

The Gospels and early Christian thought were articulated in a milieu that included many competing views of the self, the body, and salvation. The Greeks saw the body and spirit as separate things. In this sense they were a bit like Hindus, who believe that a spirit is something that might enter into another body and that a young person can have an old soul.

But in the Hebrew thought that most formed the imaginations of the writers of the New Testament, the body and the soul were inseparable. For most Hebrew teachers, both ended at death and began with the first breath of life. Remember the debates between the Sadducees and the Pharisees in the New Testament? The Sadducees believed a person died and that was it. The Pharisees believed in the resurrection of the dead. Neither would have imagined a disembodied soul in the Greek sense. If there would be eternal life, it would have to come from the resurrection of the person, the whole package: body and spirit. I could understand all this intellectually, in my mind. But I needed a way to accept in my body this idea of an integrated self.

Racing the 140.6 miles of the Ironman offered a kind of resurrection in the present—a way to bring my body to life and return it to the soul, integrating my flesh with my spirit. I wanted to go for such a distance because doing so would force me to experience my body as an undeniable reality. Such agonizing movement would require more than just body or will acting alone. Racing 140.6 miles would be a way to find the soul of my flesh, to discover in a new way the body I had struggled with for so long, hated and loved. It would reacquaint me with the body I had so wished would be subsumed into the beauty of a spiritual, intellectual self. It's that part of us so many want to believe is our truest self, even as we recognize that our flesh is our own and we can't get rid of it.

We are our bodies.

This Is My
Awakening Body

Despite the undeniable fact of our flesh, few of us are happy with our bodies. Every year the surveys report the same results: fewer than 10 percent of women are happy with their bodies, and an increasing number of men aren't happy with theirs, either. In case we thought body image was only the concern of women, 18 percent of adolescent boys are worried about their weight, and men represent one in four people struggling with an eating disorder, a statistic up from previous estimates of one in ten.[6]

Even among serious athletes there is constant worry about body image. Anorexia is a common problem among serious runners, even though they burn calories like gasoline and need the food. The happiness that comes with achieving a slender body is fleeting, because feeling truly happy with ourselves requires a different relationship to our bodies that no amount of crunches can create. At least that's what I found after my high school summer of starvation, when I finally got the body I thought I wanted.

My period of extreme dieting preceded what was, for me, the most dreaded time of year—that annual ritual of middle-class American life, the fall shopping trip for school clothes. My body never seemed to fit the available cuts of pants. Whatever the brand, either the waist was too large or the seat wouldn't fit over my butt. My butt is round and obvious—a "bubble butt" one girl called it in ninth grade. My grandmother always said my butt was from her genes, but those were a woman's genes, and in fact the way fat settled in my butt and thighs seemed womanly to me.

My butt was the first thing people would target if they were trying to insult or taunt me. I once heard a girl in the halls of our high school talking with a group of her friends: "Don't you hate it when a guy is really fine from the front and then when he turns around you're like: 'Oh, no!'" I assumed that she was talking about me; getting rid of my butt was my highest priority in the transformation of my body.

Losing weight didn't exactly get rid of my butt, but it did shrink it to something less obvious, something that felt less in the way. When it came time for me to shop for school clothes, I was down a couple of sizes and most pants fit me. Only the tight cowboy jeans I'd long ago written off remained beyond my reach. (Even today I could never be a skinny-jeaned hipster.) It felt good to fit into the clothes of my choice, the clothes most in style. It felt good to fit in with whomever and whatever was the current "cool."

My new body was not lost on my classmates. Their reactions were all I had hoped for when fantasizing that summer about returning to school. "You look great!" "Wow!" "You've lost weight!" The comments were addictive, driving my desire to keep on dieting. In our high school theater lobby, I came across Julia.

She grabbed my wrist. "You're getting so thin!" A couple of weeks later she brought me a cupcake. Julia was a flirtatious baker, and I'd hoped this was her sign that I was in the running for her attention.

I never ate the cupcake. Too many calories.

At church, my body found both new purpose and confusion. Most large evangelical youth groups try to entertain kids into salvation. The churches have gyms with climbing walls, hold Christian rock concerts, even stage evangelical versions of the teen Halloween horror house where the unsaved scream warnings from the eternal fires of hell. Thankfully, our church had new leadership and was moving away from all of this as I entered my junior year.

Instead, the youth group started implementing what were called Discipleship Small Groups. A group of high school boys or girls would meet together weekly with a mentor, do a Bible study, and work through the struggles of teenage life. The guys in my group mostly shared about our constant sins of lust, the occasional underage cigarette or beer, and our love for music with cursing in it. God deliver us. Occasionally, we read a book together on the Christian life. That is how I came to read *Celebration of Discipline* by Richard Foster. It was a book that changed how I saw religion and myself. It was a book that changed how I saw the body and soul.

Celebration of Discipline introduced an idea that had simply escaped me up to that point, that one must actually train to become Christlike, and a whole host of spiritual exercises are necessary to reach this goal. Foster taught that prayer, fasting, meditation, and other disciplines are key to living the Christian life, exercises that Christ himself practiced. And Foster explained exactly how each discipline works to form a person more deeply into Christlikeness. This was not some otherworldly brand of salvation that had nothing to do with day-to-day life. Foster showed me that Christianity is about how we live in the here and now.

This meant, I realized, that our bodies, and not just our spirits, were part of our lives as disciples. I began to see how Foster's spiritual disciplines bring together the body, mind, and spirit into a whole. I learned for the first time about practices that can engage the body in the spiritual life: fasting from all food for a day, positioning the body in different postures that can change the way people pray, opening hands up to receive God's grace, and dancing in celebration before God as King David once danced. In these descriptions I heard the first whispers of a call to a holistic life that centers not only on the individual spirit but on the whole person.

I began fasting, experimenting with how I could satisfy physical hunger through reading Scripture and praying. I started praying with my body, lying on the ground and offering myself to God from head to toe. I started to feel for the first time that my body had something significant to do with who I am as a person, even at the deep level of the soul. I had never been a hand raiser in worship services, a person who lifts his hands to God when a worship song pulls particularly on the body. But I began to experiment even with this uncomfortable gesture. I was praying not with just my mind and spirit, but with everything I was.

But then there was sex. I was a good evangelical kid, so I knew the dangers of sex and of all things that could possibly lead to sex. The body was a minefield. "A spark can set a forest fire." So went the wisdom of my youth-group education.

It was in sixth grade that the sex talks started in earnest. These talks were led by Dennis Rainey, who was both a member of our megachurch and the head of FamilyLife, an evangelical family organization with a regular program that aired across the country on Christian radio. Dennis Rainey felt sure that sixth grade was the key turning point for kids. Catch them in the sixth grade, he figured, and with the proper dose of fear, Christian kids could be inoculated against the dangers of premarital sex.

He was funny, engaging, and he had a knack for making us feel simultaneously intrigued and uncomfortable with his frankness about all things sexual. Key among his warnings was that sex was the inevitable result of a progression that started with a simple spark. Sex was a forest fire and, as we all had learned from Smokey the Bear, it didn't take much to get a forest fire started. Around a hundred boys and girls sat sprawled out or cross-legged across dark-toned industrial carpet, enthralled by these talks—both worried about getting burned and wowed by all of the sparks we hadn't even known existed until then.

I remember one talk more than any other. We were talking about the traps of the teenage life. To illustrate the dangers of traps, the leaders had brought in real traps: huge, spring-loaded jaw traps intended for coyotes and bears. These were labeled with words like "Pornography," "Masturbation," "Heavy Petting." I hadn't even known what "heavy petting" was in sixth grade. But, along with everyone else, I got an alluring description before that particular trap snapped shut on a broom handle, breaking it in half.

For preteens beginning to have their first sexual experiences—the unwanted arousals, those first sex dreams—the class both fueled our imaginations and made us guilty for our thoughts. Suddenly, our bodies had new feelings and urges, and we were told that these feelings and urges could find their proper outlet only in a marriage that seemed unimaginably far away. Our bodies became the objects of control—the dangerous seat of unpredictable desires. Yet our bodies often seemed to have minds of their own. It didn't take much in those days to make me sit a bit longer in my chair after a particularly graphic description of the forbidden pleasures hell-bound sinners might enjoy before being snapped in half by a bear trap.

There was some talk about the goodness of sex that could be found within the right context of marriage. In fact, we were told that sex for those who wait would be particularly good, made sweeter by the waiting. But coming out of those talks, our biggest motivation for waiting was fear. Teen sex wasn't presented as an issue of pearls before swine, a powerful reality we weren't ready for. It was an ever-ready source of AIDS, guaranteed to bring us death or illness before we could make it to the long-term pleasures of marriage. As we moved into high school, these messages were reinforced with greater and greater emphasis. Sexual ethics were couched as abstinence education, rather than love education. Our youth group's summer camp included a lecture and slides of swollen sex organs shown under fluorescent lighting. Hideous, gonorrhea-infected penises would be ours if we didn't watch it.

The best option presented to us was waiting. Waiting not only for sex but also for all the sparks that might lead to it. No kissing; no full-frontal hugs. Better not to date at all. Best to "court." We heard lots of stories about chaste heroes who made it all the way to their weddings without so much as kissing.

Wendell Berry, the writer and philosopher farmer, once remarked in an interview, "It seems to me that God and sex ought to be talked about a great deal less than they are; the intimate things of life ought not to be talked glibly about."[7] He could have been talking about my church, where we talked confidently and incessantly about both, never with the tenuous awe people should keep when facing the sacred. The result was that I wasn't fully prepared for the inevitability of strange and disruptive engagements with both sex and God. God was presented in church as a clear reality, one whose will was somehow unmysterious. To unveil that will, we were told, all we needed to do was read more of the Bible. But when I tried this, I did not find clear answers but a book that was full of struggles with the sacred; of people who somehow made it through a bewildering mix of cultural mores and bad sexual ethics, yet somehow connected with God at the end.

We talked little about connection those days in youth group. With God and with sex, the key words were *obedience, morality, authority.* We could easily have asked in the words of that Tina Turner song:

"What's love got to do with it?" Sure we talked about love. But it wasn't that lost-in-another kind of love—the erotic, desiring love that had historically marked Christian mysticism. We were rarely taught that sex is about connection as much as it is about pleasure, and so we lost the fullness of its goodness and implicitly adopted the same messed-up view of sexuality promoted by mass culture. Sex was just about pleasure, the self-seeking mutual masturbation of sitcom TV where characters simply use each other for their own satisfaction. It just had to be done in the context of marriage rather than after a singles-bar pickup.

Rob Bell writes about the real nature of sexuality in his book *Sex God*. "We're severed and cut off and disconnected in a thousand ways, and we know it, we feel it, we're aware of it every day," he writes. For Bell, this is the reality we all live in as human beings. Sexuality is about this disconnection and our longing to heal it. "Our sexuality is our awareness of how profoundly we're severed and cut off and disconnected," Bell writes. "Our sexuality is [also] all of the ways we go about trying to reconnect."[8]

Wendell Berry was right to speak of God and sex together. They are the most sacred things in life because both are tied to this essential connection that life is all about. The first is our lover and the second, the connector to that love. When we engage intimately with the otherness of another's body, we are engaged in some small way in the otherness of God. We are giving and we are being given to: the ultimate connection with the Ultimate. That provides plenty of reason not to go sleeping around, not to take sex lightly, without resorting to arguments based on fear. We church kids tried to keep away from sex, not because of a greater love, but because of the closing bear trap.

But there were these girls that I longed for in their flesh and warmth. Confident in my new thinness, I met them, went on dates, parked in empty places with wild red sunsets. I discovered things about the body that I'd never known—that an earlobe is electric, that there are nerves in the neck that run the length of the body. This was a truth I could feel and touch and see. This was a truth I could taste and exchange, flesh with flesh.

If the trap was there, it seemed worth the risk. The spirit is willing but the flesh is weak. Or maybe the spirit is weak and the flesh is willing. Whichever it is, I found myself divided again. My spirit was searching for new transcendence in prayer and meditation while my body was wrapped up in the electric, earthbound experiences of first kisses and backseat revelations. I didn't know how to put it all together. I felt that I had to decide: sacrifice the body to the spirit or the spirit to the body. I stood confused before the altar of false choice like Abraham with Isaac, waiting for an angel to show me another way.

16 Weeks to Ironman

4:30 p.m.
Downtown Athletic Club

I left work thirty minutes ago and already my shirt is drenched with sweat. I stand on the runners of the treadmill, my legs wide, the belt speeding below me. I breathe deep and hold myself up by the rails as I lift my legs and lower my body down. When my feet hit the belt, my neurons snap and fire and my muscles and tendons contract in an all-out sprint. My heart feels as if it is going to be ripped out; my legs threaten to cramp. I try to calm my breath and mind. *Our Father in heaven, hallowed be thy name, thy kingdom come, thy will be done...* "Amen" comes just as I hit the quarter-mile mark. I jump onto the runners again and wipe my face with a towel, watching the clock run down the rest interval until it hits forty-five seconds, then: *Run!*

If you can watch television while you're on the treadmill, you aren't running hard enough. No matter how loud the gym has Fox News playing, however enthralling you might find the hundredth rerun of *NCIS,* you should be running so hard that all your attention is focused on staying on the belt. If what you want is a slow walk, a jog, a long run, then go outside, get some vitamin D, and enjoy the scenery. Whoever thought of putting televisions in gyms wasn't interested in promoting anyone's health. Televisions just encourage the idea that running is a chore to be distracted from, rather than a pleasure to be experienced.

If you want to run, then make your run entertaining. Run down a wooded trail and imagine some primal enemy chasing you. Run for your life. Imagine a deer running in front of you and run it down; that's how our ancestors hunted, running animals to exhaustion. Remember that the deer can't sweat; you can catch it if you go long enough. Use your imagination. Do whatever you can think of to make running fun. A television in front of a treadmill? That's like a ball for a gorilla in the zoo: entertainment in the cage.

I hate the treadmill, but there are times when I need it—not so much for my legs and lungs but for my mind and even my spirit. If I go to the local track and run repeats around it, I am prone to slow down, to back off on the fourth repeat even though I have three more to go. My body could take it. I could run harder than I do. But my mind has this powerful way of saying, *Slow down. Stop. You're going too hard.* That's where the treadmill comes in.

On a treadmill I can turn the dial to just above what I already know I can do. Five-minute repeats with a minute-thirty rest in between. I set the pace at a six-minute mile—a fast pace for me, one I know I'll struggle maintaining and would have a hard time keeping up around a track. *Lift, fall, lift, fall.* My mind can keep track only of the movement of my legs, my every breath. My body takes all the focus I can bring to it. I try to keep my head neutral and my shoulders relaxed, my back straight. The clock ticks down until the run interval is over. I keep watching it but try not to. Somehow I make it through the five minutes at a pace that's faster than I can run. And then I do it again, and again. *And again.* This is what a treadmill is for. It's a way to break through the mental barrier I put on myself. It is a way of overcoming the central governor, that little dictator in my brain.

The Central Governor Theory is the idea that the mind and not the body determines the absolute limit of athletic performance in endurance racing. It's a concept famously proposed by Tim Noakes, a South African physiologist, running guru, and iconoclast. Noakes is known for his massive book *Lore of Running*, a thousand-plus-page summary of everything worth knowing about running, from physiology to a training plan for running fifty kilometers (which Noakes has done several times). You'd be hard pressed to find a serious running coach who doesn't own a copy.

Noakes has also become known for challenging the healthiness of high-carbohydrate diets and the perceived need for sodium supplementation during endurance events. Good-bye, Gatorade. But Noakes isn't just out to challenge tradition; he's a serious scientist who wants to question the conventional wisdom and follow the best research. This is what brought him to question the limits of aerobic capacity.

The conventional understanding that you'll hear from most coaches and physiologists is that the upper limit for performance in an endurance athlete is determined by aerobic fitness. By this reasoning, the winner of the Tour de France is the person who has the greatest aerobic capacity (or the most efficient mix of drugs, but that's a different issue). The fastest runner in the New York City Marathon is the one with the ability to get the most oxygen to his muscles at the highest speed. This measure of aerobic fitness is typically expressed as VO^2 max ("Vee-oh-two max," as athletes say it).

In order for your muscles to efficiently produce all of the contractions necessary to run or bike or swim, your body must deliver oxygenated blood to those muscles. To test the maximum limit of the body's ability to deliver oxygen, an athlete is put on a stationary bike or treadmill and fitted with a face mask that will help measure and test oxygen utilization. As the athlete runs or cycles, the speed or difficulty is increased gradually so that she will have to work harder and harder.

At first athletes are able to increase their oxygen usage. But eventually oxygen utilization plateaus, and they can continue running or cycling no longer. Much of their VO^2 max numbers are determined by genetics, but most people can increase their VO^2 max approximately 15 percent through training. Whatever your VO^2 max is, the conventional thinking goes, that's the limit of your endurance performance. Except it isn't.

Tim Noakes and his colleagues in Cape Town tested the VO^2 max of a group of trained athletes over several visits to his lab. During the initial visits, they conducted the standard VO^2 max tests. As the treadmill speeds increased, athletes eventually reached plateaus and the tests were over. They had reached their VO^2 max.

But on the fourth test the scientists tricked the participants. The scientists started the test at a speed higher than what the athletes had achieved incrementally in the earlier tests, then decreased the speed from there. The athletes were expecting the test to get harder, so they ran the first part of the test at a level that took them beyond their VO^2 max—what was supposed to be the upper limit of their aerobic capacity. What Noakes and his colleagues demonstrated was that the limit of VO^2 max represents not a purely physical limit, but also a psychological one.

In an interview with triathlete and podcast host Ben Greenfield, Noakes explained what this means for athletes in the context of racing: "What we used to say is the guy who comes second hasn't trained hard enough and they put too much lactic acid in his heart; he's not pumping enough oxygen, and so on and so forth." With that view, the answer for the second-place athlete would be to simply train harder.

But Noakes suggests that based on his research, we should be asking different questions: What was it in the runner's emotional makeup that came out of his childhood and his training and how he sees himself, that caused him to come in second? The difference between the first-place guy and the second-place guy probably isn't a few extra laps in the pool or more time spent running on the track. Noakes concludes, "It's not training and it's not physiology that makes you come second.... It is a mental choice you make, probably at the subconscious level."[9]

There's a video on YouTube that illustrates this difference between first and second, which I like to watch to get pumped up for a race. The video shows the final two minutes of a triathlon World Cup championship, Eminem's "Lose Yourself" blasting in the background. The camera focuses in on three runners. Suddenly one of them, Kris Gemmell, starts sprinting from the back to the front, putting more and more distance on his competitors. He's focused, his face determined, but he keeps looking back. He keeps checking on the progress of the other runners. Just before the end, Bevan Docherty begins to close ground. As he passes Gemmell, you can see that Gemmell doesn't have enough desire to catch him. Docherty's face is contorted in a grimace. Everything he has, the whole of his person, is focused on the finish line. He wins.

Docherty is known for these kinds of finishes. His motto, often repeated, is "He who wants it most wins." Docherty understands the mental aspect of triathlon. He knows that the difference between him and Gemmell isn't one of fitness. The outcome of that race wasn't determined by two athletes' physical potential. The deciding factor was that Docherty was able to push his body more, to bring the entirety of his person to the goal of winning.

This difference is a matter of the brain and spirit, and it is something that can be trained, according to Noakes. The way to train for that kind of finish is to spend a lot of time training at high intensity, a lot of time reminding your brain that your body can do more than it thinks. If Noakes's Central Governor Theory is right, then to race well we have to build grit as well as muscle, determination as much as lung capacity.

It's for my character as much as my body that I keep training on the treadmill. This is a workout that makes me bring my all. On race day it won't be only my body that matters, but my whole self.

This Is My College Body

Weaton College: "Evangelical Vatican" to some, alma mater of Billy Graham and the missionary martyr Jim Elliot, with a motto of "Faith Seeking Understanding" (the celebration of the Christian intellectual life), prayer before every class, and three-times-a-week chapel. No drinking, no smoking, no dancing. That is the official party line at Wheaton, the image of some holy place set on a hill.

But that's not the real place. The real Wheaton is fundamentalist students who play in praise bands and want to be missionaries but end up being drawn into a cult led by a con-artist graduate student who'd been invited to speak from the chapel stage. It's girls who want to make out, who feel guilty when they do, and won't talk to the guy afterward, then do it all over again. It's boys who share in small groups their struggles with sexual temptation and can't seem to control themselves around their Christian "sisters." The real Wheaton is college professors who subvert the administration, who edge up to the line (sometimes crossing over it), and occasionally get fired, triggering protests by hundreds of students. The real Wheaton is a place of contradictions and contrasts, deep learning and surprising spirituality—a place where God shows up in strange settings.

God showed up in conversations I had late at night as I smoked cigarettes and walked with friends through the eerie quiet of the Chicago suburbs, the fall fog hanging in the air, porch lights spreading into the dark like an empty welcome. God showed up the summer after my sophomore year when I met a girl in the heart of Chicago who had come to God through reading the Bible and Kierkegaard at a secular liberal-arts school. She went to church with me once and trembled through the service, full of awe and fear. Through her, I saw just how power-filled this thing I'd been doing all my life really was.

God showed up when I first tried to meditate and pray with a rosary, my hands moving over the beads without my mind knowing the words. During one quiet night spent practicing this ritual, I felt a strong sense of an unseen presence, as if Jesus was there in the room with me, in body. God showed up as I read Nietzsche's *Thus Spoke Zarathustra* alongside the gospel of Mark, an experience that illustrated for me that Jesus was not unlike Nietzsche's hero, the "superman" who would come and redefine what it means to be human, overthrowing the old law tables.

Wheaton was a place where I felt like I didn't fit, but did. I didn't fit the images from the front of the school catalogue or the official party line. Yet most people there didn't fit. It was an institution caught between a past and a present that were at odds. As freshmen, we came in thoroughly evangelical; conservative fundamentalists, mostly. But many of us left something else: Episcopalian, Eastern Orthodox, Catholic, atheist, agnostic. There were those who came away unchanged, simply more-educated evangelicals. But I didn't know many like that. Most students changed their tradition or went outside the faith.

Some Wheaton grads came to appreciate the strange time they spent there. Others still can't make sense of it. There's a Facebook "recovery" group for students through the generations who didn't, or couldn't, toe the line. They are the "Wheaton College Pledge Breaking Society International" — a group of students who drank, smoked, or simply danced while at Wheaton. Most former students agree that the best experiences were often unofficial and extracurricular, or something that could get a student or professor on the administration's bad side.

The professors were often excellent. These were the teachers who introduced me to Toni Morrison and Flannery O'Connor; showed me radical experiments in form like the heartbreaking, newly ascendant graphic novel *Jimmy Corrigan: The Smartest Kid on Earth;* and exposed me to the movies of Andrei Tarkovsky, which still haunt me as the most powerful icons of faith ever recorded on film. One professor was always available for lunchtime conversations about the philosophers Derrida and Gadamer; another taught a course on the philosophy of pragmatism that has had a profound impact on how I think about truth itself.

While these professors still loom large in my mind, the events that most marked my time in college happened off campus. I often hung out at Gourmand, a coffee shop on Printer's Row in the South Loop of Chicago that was painted Matisse-red and had high ceilings. The stereo played a mix that one barista called "seductive coffee shop," a playlist of Portishead and Bowery Electric and Massive Attack. It was a place where students, real-deal writers, and real-deal artists would hang out, smoking and talking together in an environment that felt more like 1920s Paris than turn-of-the-millennium Chicago. A group of us would take the train there to study — a forty-five-minute ride on the Metra rail to downtown, then a fifteen-minute walk. This was our escape. There we could fantasize about being writers and philosophers, smoke expensive cigarettes from France and England, and study our textbooks about the theologies of Tillich and Barth, Augustine and Aquinas.

I had never smoked so much as a cigar or had a taste of beer before

Wheaton. In high school, I had never run in the crowds that did those things, and I had no desire for them. But in the city I felt drawn to the look and the feel of both. And I loved the taste. I came to understand the power of alcohol with its flavor and warmth. I enjoyed the cool of sitting in a bar with a cigarette in hand, a glass of wine in front of me, as I conversed with classmates about Foucault and French post-structuralism. This was in part a kind of literary act. My friends and I hunted for old, famous bars like the Rainbow Room in Wicker Park, where Nelson Algren had gone to drink. Writers and cigarettes and bars seem to go together, for better or worse.

Of course I wasn't supposed to smoke or drink. Those acts were prohibited by the previously mentioned college pledge, which applied off campus as much as it did on. This wasn't anything I'd thought about when I signed it as a part of the admissions process. But sometime around my sophomore year, I started to be a pledge breaker.

These were the two sides of Wheaton. On one side were the rule followers, and on the other were the rule breakers; the people who toed the evangelical and institutional line, and those who stretched and challenged it, theologically or morally, or both. The challengers were often serious about faith, more serious at times than the compliers.

There was Thomas who studied theology, read deeply, and prayed with incredible discipline, and also used his smoking habit as a way to open up conversations with the male prostitutes and drug addicts with whom he'd share a cigarette. Then there were the people like Chad who walked barefoot around campus in even the coldest weather, hung out with the homeless on weekends, and challenged the rest of us to live for the poor. Andy, an ex-con who'd experienced a prison conversion to Christianity and had become a radical pacifist, introduced us to Mennonite traditions and the teachings of peace theologians like John Howard Yoder. He memorized the whole Sermon on the Mount while drinking a rum and Coke in his dorm room.

The opposing sides of Wheaton life often clashed on the Forum Wall, a brick structure just past the mailboxes in the student center. On the Forum Wall, students posted articles, essays, and manifestos. There were responses to chapel talks and opinion essays on the news of the day. Other students answered by writing in the margins of the items that had been posted, like analog Facebook comments. Sometimes a student wrote and posted an entire counter-essay, debates raging on for weeks. For the most part, what was posted on the Forum Wall—whatever it was, however offensive—was sacrosanct. Tearing down a post was anathema.

Inevitably every spring the Forum Wall became host to a debate about tank tops. It usually started with some freshman newly emerged from high school youth group, bearing all the guilt that comes with living in an eighteen-year-old's body. He was feeling lust, and he figured the problem had to be with the women and their skin.

Dear Sisters in Christ,

As warm weather comes please be considerate of your male classmates. We try to see you in a godly way, but when you wear tank tops and short shorts it makes that difficult for us. When you dress, please help us to see you in a holy and pure way.

Sincerely,
Your Brother in Christ

Next came the responses. One art student posted an illustration of herself naked, her backpack on her shoulders.

"Is this how you see me walking around campus?" she asked, putting the problem back on the male gaze—the undressing of women in the mind. Another female student would then defend the original post, arguing that "sisters" don't really understand how much their wardrobe choices affect their brothers in Christ. After a time the debate would die out. Girls, for the most part, kept wearing tank tops and showing their legs. Still, the conversation revealed the view held by many Christians that lust and shame and guilt are caused by women's bodies and not by men's attitudes and choices toward them; that the problem is just tank tops, just the fact of breasts and legs. The cause of all lust lay in a woman's body.

I'd heard messages along that line often enough. In youth group, at summer camp, and in Christian teen magazines the message was often repeated that boys and men were beings whose overpowering sexual drive simply couldn't be controlled and women were emotionally hungry Jezebels willing to trade sex or its promise for easy affirmation. The solution presented was for women to control their bodies: access, dress, and purity. It was her responsibility to keep the gaze of men away from her; it was up to her to remain a pure, undefiled bride on her wedding night.

Of course, there were things that the "brothers" could do to help their sisters. One of my summer camp counselors advised us boys on how to resist lust: "Just find something about a girl that is really ugly, like a pimple or mole or something, and focus on that."

I found a better response in Walt Whitman's poem "I Sing the Body Electric."

I sing the body electric,
The armies of those I love engirth me and I engirth
    them,
They will not let me off till I go with them, respond to
    them,
And discorrupt them, and charge them full with the
    charge of the soul.

Was it doubted that those who corrupt their own
      bodies conceal themselves?
And if those who defile the living are as bad as they
      who defile the dead?
And if the body does not do fully as much as the soul?
And if the body were not the soul, what is the soul?[10]

This shaming of the body I witnessed at Wheaton was a kind of defilement, a denigration of the holy beauty of the body. At the heart of this shaming was a separation, as there is in every kind of defilement. Students still felt a sense that for the body to be pure its desires must be pushed down, even if the real problem lay not in the body but in the spirit.

I wondered: *Why not respond to the beauty of an attractive person with amazement and praise to the Creator of that body, like one would about a waterfall or a gazelle?* (A gazelle was, after all, a favored biblical metaphor for a sexually attractive person.) The problem lay in the way we had been brought up to see the body—as the shell of the real person inside it. But what if the body is the soul, as Whitman suggests?

The body and the soul—equal, a part of one another, a whole. Whitman saw that somehow their destruction was contained in their separation; that to see the body as not being tied up with the soul is to see the soul as unbound and unmoored. This was the way I had grown up thinking. It was the same way of seeing that led to those Forum Wall comments that explained lechery as a sin that originated from a woman's body. This is the line of thinking that tells us our souls are what matter and the body is just a dangerous distraction that can lead us to lust and gluttony and, from there, into all kinds of other sins.

I was sitting in a class on the philosophy of science when I began to recognize that this understanding, so common in our culture—Christian and otherwise—was not simply given to us from the Bible. In my reading for that course, I came across German theologian Oscar Cullmann's *On the Immortality of the Soul.* Here I first encountered the idea that an eternal soul and finite body were really Greek conceptions that had been introduced to and imposed on Christianity.

The idea of an immortal soul separate from the body would have been alien to the Hebrew way of thinking. When David prays to God he asks for life because "in death there is no remembrance of you; in Sheol who can give you praise?" (Psalm 6:5). The wisdom teacher of Ecclesiastes writes: "The living know that they will die, but the dead know nothing; they have no more reward, and even the memory of them is lost" (9:5). To die, in the ancient Hebrew understanding, was a kind of final act. The dead were dead, not continuing on after bodily life in some spiritual form. The only hope for return was the full return of both body and soul.

This can be a terrifying thought, particularly in our culture that focuses so much on the life of the individual. But like many ancient cultures, the Hebrews focused more on being a people than on individual lives. The continuation of the self was less important than the salvation and continuation of the people of God. I'd grown up with both an individualistic idea of immortality and an individualistic view of salvation. I knew that church community was important and all. But that community was important for *my* walk with God, my *personal* relationship with Jesus. Now, in college, I felt unsettled by Cullmann's argument that Greeks had been the source of the eternal-soul and finite-body paradigm. This told me that the immortality of the person hadn't been as important to the ancient Israelites as had been the immortality of God's people as a whole. I faced a new question: If, like the Hebrews, believers today thought that we just died at the end of our lives, how would that change our view of church?

Cullmann further argued that if we want to find a source for the idea of a separate soul and body, we should look not to the Scriptures but to Plato and his teacher Socrates. Socrates on his deathbed tells his disciple Crito not to worry because his soul will go on: "Be of good cheer, then, my dear Crito, and say that you are burying my body only."[11] Death in the Greek conception was a friend; it was a liberation of the true self from the chains of the body.

But in Christianity, Death is a force that is opposed to God. Death is an enemy to be defeated. This is not simply death as the end of life, but the force of Death: the unraveling and dissolution of the creation. It is this Death that Christ finally defeats through his own death and proclaims to be ended through his resurrection. "Where, O death, is your sting?" Paul taunts in the light of resurrection, even as he is ready to face his own mortal end (1 Corinthians 15:55).

And here is where Christianity diverges from some of the ancient Hebrew views of individual death. Christians, like it or not, are Pharisees. Pharisees differed from other religious leaders in the days of Jesus and Paul by insisting on a physical resurrection from the dead. Like them, Christians believe that the people of God will one day live restored in body and soul on an earth that is returned to God's intention. Death is an enemy *because the body matters.* If the body were just some vehicle that could be cast off for another when it breaks down, there would be no need for resurrection. If the body doesn't matter, then we could just go through a series of reincarnations, re-enfleshments of the self.

But in Christianity the incarnation of Christ is a singular event. Each person's incarnation is a singular event. Resurrection of the singular incarnation of one's self is the only hope of life beyond death.

"He has now reconciled [you] in his fleshly body," the writer of Colossians says (1:22). It is the body that makes the Cross important; it is in Christ's flesh, not his soul, that Christians should hope. If Christ simply died and his soul went on to heaven, then there wouldn't be any Easter. There wouldn't be any hope of our own resurrection.

Christian bishop Augustine of Hippo had once been a Platonist and a Manichean: a follower of a religion that taught that the spirit was good and the body a source of evil. Later as a Christian, Augustine wrote and preached in celebration of the body that he once rejected. One Easter season around the turn of the fifth century, Augustine took on the pagan philosophies of his day that denigrated the body. Answering the pagan philosopher Porphyry, who argued that "every kind of body must be avoided," Augustine preached:

> According to the teaching of God, our faith praises the body,
> because, although we draw punishment for sin from the body
> which we now possess, and although "the corruptible body is a
> load upon the soul," nevertheless, the body has its own beauty,
> its own arrangement of members, its differentiation of senses, its
> erect posture, and other qualities which evoke the admiration of
> those considering it. Furthermore, it is destined to be completely
> incorruptible, completely immortal, completely agile and quick
> in movement.[12]

Christian faith, Augustine realized, cannot reject the body. It must instead celebrate it in anticipation of our re-creation through resurrection. Christ came in the flesh, Christ rose in the flesh, and Christ will redeem us in the flesh. Today when we praise the body, admiring its beauty as Augustine suggested, we are honoring the Creator. Our problem is not our bodies but in the disordered self that is trapped in this reality we call sin, the Fall, our state of corruption.

If I'd been singing "the body electric" as a youth group praise song, I might have been better prepared for the realities of my maturing body and celebrated it rather than felt divided by it. Perhaps cultivating this kind of attitude could have helped me and other teens suffering from a host of bodily troubles from anorexia to steroids, a growing problem among young men. How would it have looked if, instead of staring at photos of gonorrheal genitals, we had wondered together at images of the amazingly beautiful body created by Christian Renaissance artists: God's creation of our flesh?

"Cover your skin; cover your face," some argue. "It's just a body," others say. But if the body and soul are two parts of the same whole, this changes how we relate to both. Both become sacred and free in a way that neither finger-wagging fundamentalists nor pornographers could ever understand.

My rational understanding of the connections between body and spirit was sparked during my study of philosophy and theology. But it was in church that they became a part of me. At Wheaton going to church was a given—the only question was, which one? Churches in the area advertised their programs; they brought vans to make the trip easier, lining them up outside of the cafeteria to catch students as they emerged after breakfast.

I moved from church to church every Sunday, to congregations running the gamut from the hyper-Calvinist College Church to the radical Jesus People USA in Chicago, where old hippies and young punk rockers live together in a commune and death-metal bands play after the baby dedication. These experiences were all important in broadening my view of the church. I eventually settled into St. Mark's Episcopal Church in Glen Ellyn, one suburb over from Wheaton—a place that welcomed college students but did nothing to advertise to them.

The church I grew up in had been built with all of the temporary beauty of a shopping mall. Outside, it was covered in metal siding. Inside, the aesthetics were plain and generic. When the time came for the church to move to a new campus, having exhausted its already sprawling space, few modifications were needed to make the building suitable for the secular prep school that bought it. The space and place meant little in both practice and theology, a fitting approach given their teachings that it is the immortal soul, and not the body, that really matters.

In the Episcopal church, I found a world where the life of the spirit was embodied: physically present in the buildings, the prayer books and hymnals, the bread and wine of holy communion, the oil of healing and confirmation, and the changing vestments—priestly garb—of the liturgical seasons. The very shape of the building, stonework in an English country style with a traditional nave, was meant to instruct us. Alan Jacobs, a literature professor at Wheaton and member of the church, helped teach the confirmation class for new members, revealing all of the rich textures and hidden meanings of the building and prayer books in the same way he helped students explore the many layers of James Joyce's *Ulysses* and W. H. Auden's poetry.

He taught us that the nave, the main body of the church where congregants sit for a service, is patterned after an upside-down ship recalling Noah's ark. The arching ceiling is the hull. The pews represent where the rowers would be, down in the galley, working with their bodies to propel the ship forward. The congregation is not a mere audience; everybody must do his or her part on this ark of salvation, participating in the public work of the liturgy.

At the front of the building is the sanctuary—the space for the Eucharist, where the body and blood are transformed from bread and wine. All attention, the whole orientation of the building, is directed toward the table of thanksgiving. For that is what *Eucharist* means: "thanksgiving." This central placement of the Eucharistic table testifies that the most important act done in the church is drinking the wine and eating the bread of communion.

In the Episcopal church, the pulpit of the church, the place where sermons are delivered and Scripture is read, is located to the side of the sanctuary. Sermons and Scripture reading are recognized as holy acts, but they are not the central reason for gathering. This was in sharp contrast to the churches in which I'd grown up. In my previous experience, the sermon was always delivered from the center of the stage. This, I learned, follows the tradition begun by Protestant reformers who'd wanted to emphasize the primacy of the words of Scripture over the flesh of communion. Holy Communion was important, such preachers held, but it was a mere symbol, in many cases a nonessential that fell in importance well behind the reading and preaching of the Word of God.

But in the Episcopal church, as well as in the Catholic, Lutheran, and Orthodox churches, we remember that the Word of God was made flesh and so we cannot separate the Word from flesh. It is that flesh which renders meaning to the Scriptures, and so communion is critical. Martin Luther, the founding Protestant, was adamant that Eucharist be central to worship, claiming: "The glory of our God is precisely that for our sakes he comes down to the very depths, into human flesh, into the bread, into our mouth, our heart, our bosom."[13] Luther used the term "Enthusiasts" to describe John Calvin, Huldrych Zwingli, and other reformers who rejected the idea that Christ was really present in the bread and wine of communion, saying, "Before I would drink mere wine with the Enthusiasts, I would rather have pure blood with the Pope."[14] If you've ever read Luther's comments on the pope, you'll understand how strongly he felt about Christ's real presence in the Eucharist.

Such an elevation of the Eucharist was a strange transition for me. Growing up, communion had been a once-a-month affair performed with little saltine crackers and grape juice. I even saw it once performed with Goldfish crackers. Communion was a symbol and, though we were told it was an important one, the implicit message was that it was not nearly as important as what we did when we read Scripture. That communion had been the central gathering activity of the early church was completely lost to me.

At St. Mark's, the words of the Eucharistic service were printed in a little book called *The Book of Common Prayer* that sat in a rack in the back of pews, giving a physicality to the words of the service. In those books, with the stains and oily fingerprints, I found a kind of memory—a physical reminder of those who had once held that same book and prayed those same prayers before me. In the same way we sang hymns from the hymnal, which was a strange experience for me after years of reading song lyrics projected onto megachurch walls. But a few Sundays spent fumbling through the hymnal and *The Book of Common Prayer* was worth the deep connection with the physical books that came to me in time.

My roommate John, a brilliant math and philosophy double major who had come from the most extreme sort of fundamentalist home, joined the Episcopal church at the same time, and we began a practice of saying Morning Prayer together. I had no idea then what I was starting, but I have been saying those same prayers from *The Book of Common Prayer* off and on for over a decade now; this has been my most consistent faith practice. John and I knelt when the book said to kneel, stood when the book said to stand, sat when the book said to sit. We found that these were not regimented practices, but rather postures that best put us into the position of prayer. We discovered that it wasn't only what we said with our words but what we did with our bodies that made up the full act of praying to God.

We learned by heart the common prayers: the Lord's Prayer, the

Confession, the Nicene and Apostles' Creeds, the Great Thanksgiving. By memorizing these prayers we made them a part of our bodies, neurons and neurochemicals creating patterns in the gray matter of our brains for those memories. Though I'd grown up in church all my life, I didn't even know the Lord's Prayer before college. Form prayers and creeds were completely absent from my upbringing. Now I was embodying them.

To embody Scripture and prayer is to live them. Literary critic Brad Leithauser, in his essay "Why We Should Memorize," published in *The New Yorker* online, wrote about the need for people to memorize poems, despite their constant availability via the Internet and smartphones: "The best argument for verse memorization may be that it provides us with knowledge of a qualitatively and physiologically different variety: you take the poem inside you, into your brain chemistry if not your blood, and you know it at a deeper, bodily level than if you simply read it off a screen."[15]

John and I came to know this in our bodies; we came to live into the prayers of the Episcopal church, to take on its physical postures. The words worked themselves into our cells, became a part of our bodies. We knelt and bowed and crossed ourselves; we ate bread and wine that, even in their small quantities, became a part of our cells. The Episcopal church, in our early college years, became a part of us as much as we became a part of it.

In this way, I began to make sense of my body and soul together, even amid all of the confusion around me. But the confusion within that drove me to a church far from fundamentalist evangelicalism also helped to reveal an emptiness inside of me. That emptiness drove both my spiritual and physical hunger. My body had not yet learned to be satisfied with the bread of the Eucharist or the wine of communion; my soul had not found its satisfaction in Christ's living water. I found that

I wanted more—more of everything, more without limits. That hunger didn't start with food; it was a movable craving, an appetite that sent me searching for something that would fill it.

I came to realize that although I didn't love the emptiness—the hole inside me that longed for fulfillment—I did love the craving. Spiritually, I was like the classical Romans who would vomit their food in the course of the meal, denying the limits of their body in order to keep eating. I never went so far as to practice this kind of bulimia, either spiritually or physically, but I did let the craving of my desires replace the fulfillment for which they were intended. I was off center, disordered, and dissonant in body and soul. I didn't want to be full because I would have to stop eating.

Ironman as a Spiritual Discipline

I call Sister Madonna Buder because, as an octogenarian nun and athlete, she might, I hope, have some words to offer me in my quest to unite body and soul. When I reach her on the phone, she tells me that she's just back from a thirty-mile bike ride. The Ironman 70.3 Eagleman triathlon is coming up, she says, and she plans to try there to qualify once again for the Ironman World Championship in Kona, Hawaii. The year before, Sister Madonna became the oldest person to ever finish a 140.6-mile race, crossing the finish line at Ironman Canada at age eighty-two. She laughs as she says, "Everyone was congratulating me about my world record. I didn't know what they were talking about!" Sister Madonna Buder doesn't race for the record books.

Sister Madonna didn't start triathlons or even running until the middle of her life, over twenty years after she first took her vows as a monastic. At a spiritual retreat she attended, a priest spoke of running as "a way to integrate mind, body, and spirit."

"I've always been a holistic person," Sister Madonna tells me, "and I love to be in creation; it is so healing. So I started running to be out in it."

I had never thought about my own beginning bike rides and runs as a way of being in creation, but her words made me realize that, in many ways, this was what drew me to triathlon. Every day of training is a day spent riding on country roads, running down park paths, or swimming in fog-draped lakes. But it is more than that for her and for me; it is also a way to *embrace* our creation. By using our bodies, pushing them to their limits, we embrace our *createdness* and in this we offer a kind of praise to the Creator who gifted us with these muscles and lungs and hearts.

Her first race was a prayer of intercession. After she'd begun running as a spiritual discipline, she saw a poster in Spokane advertising the annual Bloomsday run: a 12K that attracts as many as fifty thousand runners.

"I thought they were crazy," she says. But soon afterward her mother called and said that one of her brothers was having marital problems rooted in his alcoholism.

"I told myself: 'I'm going to do the Bloomsday race as a way of interceding for my brother.' My intention was to ask the Lord to take my will to endure these eight miles and transfer this determination to my brother, that he might acquire the will to abstain from his habit." She ran and she endured and she felt God's blessing through the miles of running for her brother's healing.

Her introduction to triathlon came years later. Like many runners she longed for a new challenge, and a friend suggested she take on a triathlon race. She signed up for a sprint race, and like her first running race, she made her first triathlon an intercession. She has three brothers and used each of the three legs of the race to pray for them. Since that first triathlon in 1982, Sister Madonna has competed in over 360 triathlons, forty-five of which were Ironman races. Those races continue to be prayers for her; the long runs and rides and swims acting as meditations on the Trinity of God as well as on a trinity within herself. When she runs, she says, "It's the trinity working together: mind, body, and soul."

The danger comes, she tells me, "when we overindulge any one of those aspects, like the physical. Then we are not complete." A complete picture of God, in the Christian view, can't be limited to the Father or the Son or the Holy Spirit. God is a community, and it is only in this community that God is love, each person of the Trinity offering itself to the others. We need the three persons of the Trinity to live in the fullness of God.

I realize as Sister Madonna speaks that before I started running I'd been experiencing this problem with my body. I'd been out of balance, leaning too much on my spirit or too much on my mind. What I needed were all three working in harmony; as she had, I was beginning to find in triathlon a way toward that balance.

"We have a spark of divinity in us made in the image and likeness of God," Sister Madonna explains. That spark of divinity, that image and likeness, isn't a matter of just the spirit or mind. It is also a matter of the body. Sister Madonna has found that again and again while enduring the 140.6 miles of the Ironman, finishing before the clock cuts off at seventeen hours. Finishing before the clock cuts off—that's the reality of the race and of our lives. We only have so much time to run this race. At some point the clock will run to its limit. Sister Madonna lives in this awareness, spiritually and physically, and she savors the miles she still has.

"When I'm out running or biking...I drink in the wonder of creation." She speaks with marvel in her voice, the awe of one more run. Like her, the more rides I go on, the more runs I take, the more afternoons I spend swimming in the open water of a lake, the more I experience this kind of wonder. Sister Madonna has become a kind of icon in the world of triathlon not just because of her physical achievement, which has continued to be record breaking, but also because in her joy she reminds us what racing should be about—joy overcoming and overwhelming the darkness within ourselves.

A good race is a celebration of human life. The Psalms say that we were made "a little lower than the angels" (8:5, NIV) and yet we do not live into that grandness. To race is to embrace this human life that began when God bent down and breathed the divine life into those first lungs, shaped from the dirt. When we race we reflect the divine pronouncement over all of creation: "God saw everything that he had made, and indeed, it was very good" (Genesis 1:31).

This Is My
Searching Body

There is pleasure to be found in a cigarette. Addictive, deadly in the wrong mix, an eventual barrier to climbing stairs or mountains, or running even a mile? Yes. But the taste, the empty satisfaction of smoke, the economy of give-and-take and sharing with other smokers—a cigarette has its virtues. The cigarette is the perfect gluttons' meal: full of flavor, empty, satisfying for only a moment. One leads to another. Just one more.

In college as I sorted out my desires, letting my body succumb to one hope after another, "one more" often came just before midnight. In the middle of a haphazard study session, my friends and I frequently felt the need for cigarettes and a box of Krispy Kreme doughnuts. This required a drive to the next suburb over. We piled into Brien's Chevy Caprice, navy blue with fuzzy dice hanging from the rearview mirror, and drove twenty minutes for the hot sugar glaze. We'd split a couple dozen doughnuts four ways and smoke a pack before we got back to the smoke-free zone of Wheaton.

"One more" provided me with a smoke screen at the nightclubs we frequented: big clubs set in warehouses where the music was too loud to talk, girls danced, and I was unable to make my body move or make sense of my being there. From the comfort of the bar I watched the shadows and shapes of the bodies on the dance floor, feeling a confusing mix of desire and disgust, shame and lust. Food and sex and alcohol—these are all common companions of the cigarette. The cigarette is the flavor of the one-night stand, the aftertaste of the hangover, the compulsive interlude of a meal. It was a kind of malicious sacrament for me—an outward sign of inward sin.

"One more" has always been my problem. Smoking wasn't a new emergence of addiction in me but the fulfillment of what had already been inside, a natural symbol of my insatiable appetite.

"There aren't enough days in your life for everything you want to do," my mother often said when I was growing up. I wanted to do, to see, to have; my curiosity was without borders. Other children wanted Happy Meals and hot dogs; I wanted the foods I'd never tried. I ordered the strangest thing I could find on any restaurant menu: emu steak or octopus or liver. I would go deep with archaeology, astronomy, paleontology—reading everything I could. When I'd reached a certain level of knowledge and mastery, I'd move on to the next thing. Time was my constant enemy, making me choose between this book or that one, this meal or another, this experience over that experience.

At college, this desire for more became unbounded from the stability of home life. Gluttony and ambition and lust mixed together: lust for holy things, lust for carnal things, lust for more of everything. Jack Kerouac's *On the Road* was a clear articulation of my life at that point: "The only people for me are the mad ones, the ones who are mad to live, mad to talk, mad to be saved, desirous of everything at the same time, the ones who never yawn or say a commonplace thing, but burn, burn, burn like fabulous yellow roman candles exploding like spiders across the stars."[16] This was the hidden mantra of my heart. I recognized myself in Sal Paradise and Dean Moriarty and all of Kerouac's lonely characters. I also saw that, despite moving forward, they never got "more." Sal Paradise never got the girl he was searching for, never settled down in that little house he wanted. Dean Moriarty, wild hero of the road, never found his father. Far from a celebration of the transient, *On the Road* is a horror novel about the never-ending highway of unsettled, exhausted desire.

One philosophy course introduced me to Søren Kierkegaard's three "stages on life's way." These are a series of dimensions of life that are not chronological in nature but are directional and hierarchical, each containing and superseding the other. The first stage is that of the aesthetic: the sensuous and immediate life. It is the life of the cigarette, the immediate pleasure of smoke that in time blows away. If the self is constituted purely in the aesthetic realm, then life becomes nothing more than a series of disconnected events, one experience after another.

The second stage is the ethical life, in which we realize that decisions always bring about consequences. This is the life of reason, of responsibility without subjectivity—a life dominated by the "ought." The ethical stage is that of the stoic, of the "good person."

Finally there is the religious life, the stage in which we find ourselves through acts of faith that establish God as the highest authority. For Kierkegaard the ultimate expression of this was Abraham's willingness on Mount Moriah to sacrifice the ethical norms of his society in order to respond to the call of God.

In college I saw Kierkegaard's stages embodied in my friends, and I felt torn by them. Henry was the aesthete, as he said himself one day, coming in after some sorry night of drinking, smoking hash, and making out with Anna, a punk-styled girl who carried in her a volatile blend of anger and sex. He was a philosophy major given to deep rambling about the latest literature or philosopher of the day. We'd just been going over Kierkegaard when he said in a tone of weary inevitability, "I feel like I'm giving in to the aesthetic life."

Henry and I first bonded during orientation week, over philosophy and the Smashing Pumpkins. Later, we took the Metra rail into downtown Chicago and searched for the Double Door, the club where the Smashing Pumpkins had gotten their start. We knew only that it was on Milwaukee Street and so ended up walking three miles, stopping along the way in the kind of strange places that can be found only by wandering, such as the revolutionary bookstore filled with posters of Mao and Lenin and Che, where a girl our age tried to get us to join the Young Communist League. Some nights other friends joined us to wander and explore. A homeless man might hit us up for change, and we'd wander with him, learning the street through someone else's eyes.

The problem with the aesthetic life is that it becomes shallow if it is pursued without regard to something that transcends it. However beautiful or pleasurable a practice may be, if it does not include soul, it is reduced to technique. There exists a kind of formal beauty: the right use of color, a pleasant combination of tones. But if there is no soul, no hope or faith behind the beauty, the beauty never opens up into the transcendent toward which the truest beauty inevitably draws us.

The aesthetic life, seemingly wrapped up in the pleasures and beauty of the world, becomes disconnected from what is beautiful. True beauty is always tied up with goodness, and when we focus on the surface level of things, we never find that deeper goodness. The aesthete lives from one experience to another—a great movie, a great show, a good smoke. But like a drug addict, over time the aesthete feels the intensity of experience diminish. More and more aesthetic experience is craved and needed. Eventually all real sense of beauty is lost. In this way I was like Henry. I couldn't wait for the next sensation that awaited me. I couldn't wait to experience the next "experimental" or "groundbreaking" art. It was all without soul, without any authentic beauty, but at the time I was enraptured by my shallow vision.

If Henry was the representative of the aesthetic life among my friends, Martin was the representative of the ethical. Martin was a year ahead of me in school but seemed and acted older than that. He was funny and smart, but he also carried with him a weary kind of sadness that reflected a life turned toward the horrors of the world. Martin had traveled a great deal and spent time in the mountains of Chiapas working with human-rights groups. He was radical, and he believed in justice for the poor above all else.

It was through Martin that I began to get a sense that the life of a Christian should be a life turned toward the Other—both God and those whose faces held the trace of the divine image. Martin immersed himself in liberation theology. His relationship with Christianity modulated and flowed, with Martin stepping in and out of belief, but his commitment to the poor was constant. Martin was a teacher, a natural mentor. He was also insecure. It was perhaps his need for affirmation that held him in the space of the ethical; the transcendent was always locked out by his need for a loud "yes" from a quiet God.

While we were in school Martin became Catholic, in part, he explained, because he wanted to have a church "to believe for" him. But even with a church to help with the believing, one must assent to its "yes" of faith. Over time that "yes" became more difficult for Martin, eventually fading not exactly to a "no" but to silence. However, the call to visit the sick, to welcome the stranger, to feed the hungry still echoed in his life and mine. He answered the "ought" of the ethical stage with duty.

The third of Kierkegaard's stages, the religious life, was embodied by many people at Wheaton, but the ones I remember best are those whose faith transcended the fundamentalism of the school. Perhaps the greatest exemplar of the religious life was Thomas, who lived with a single-hearted dedication to his faith and to the life of truth. Like Martin, Thomas became Catholic, but he did so not because he needed a church to believe on his behalf; rather, he wanted to join his "yes" with the many "yeses" present in the continuity of that tradition.

Thomas devoted himself to learning from the great spiritual masters of history. He began a reading group of these writers, dubbing it the "Dead Fathers Society." Thomas immersed himself in the life of prayer, not simply as an abstract act but also as a physical one. He drove the school's ministry van with lit votive candles in the cup holders; he prayed the Rosary and meditated before icons. He believed that Christ transformed the substance of bread and wine into his very flesh and blood. He believed that God saturated the world.

The aesthetic, the ethical, and the religious — my life was torn between these three options, not as progressive stages but as a jumble of moments. At one point, all of the smoking and drinking and longing in my life felt as if they were breaking me into a kaleidoscope of my desires. It was during this time that I had a dream that's stuck with me through all the years since.

In the dream I was at a party, a family gathering set in the towering pine woods of my early upbringing in east Texas. Children ran in the yard while the adults ate and talked and laughed inside. I stood in front of a closed glass door. On the other side of the door was Sylvia, a black-haired art major I had a crush on at the time. She was beautiful and creative and carried with her an alluring sense of some dark wound. In the dream, we were playing some kind of game through the door. Suddenly the glass door shattered, cutting her wrists, and she was dead.

In the dream, I felt deep guilt for her death; back at school, friends and family tried to console me but could not stop the guilt or the sadness I felt. One day I went for a walk along an access road. Between the road and the interstate was a field of wildflowers. I saw in the distance, coming toward me on the road, what looked like a monk wearing a brown habit with the hood up. But when he got closer the habit dropped, and instead of a monk there was a woman, alluring and siren-like.

The woman took my hand and led me into the field where, around some bend in space, we found ourselves in a room with a dresser and lamp and bed, like a hotel room. The bed was unmade and messy, and I knew that she wanted to have sex with me there. But as she moved toward the bed, I became aware that there was already a body in the bed; alive, but sleeping. When the woman realized this too, she disappeared suddenly. I became clearly aware that she was the devil and that somehow I had been saved; that the body in the bed was the body of Christ. I walked out of the room and into the field. I saw a car parked on the access road and my father running up to me to warn me that the devil was coming to seduce me.

Then I woke up.

The dream has remained with me so powerfully because, in that strange way that dreams can do, it revealed both the situation I was in and the answer I needed at that time in my life. I was caught between childhood and adulthood, and the things I was doing held all the risk of hurting someone I loved. But there was a body in the way—a body that stopped me from a final letting-go that would mean the end.

I had gone to therapy at the college's counseling center off and on, but I found explorations of family history to be unhelpful. My anxieties and neuroses seemed somehow deeper and more personal—my parents weren't at fault. Martin had read just enough Freud to play psychoanalyst and tease out of me the truth that I already knew. "You're feeling a conflict in yourself between the faith you were brought up in and the life you're living now," he said when I told him my dream.

"Yes, yes," I said. "But what is the solution?"

I sensed that the answer had something to do with that body.

Some months later in a digital video class, I was given the assignment to film a dream. I filmed a condensed version of that dream, ending with an image of the bread and wine; the body and blood of Holy Communion held high. Though I didn't recognize it fully at the time, it was that bread and wine, that body and blood, which were saving me, keeping me both from falling fully into the aesthetic life and from rejecting faith out of a rationalistic commitment to the ethical.

Few of my friends survived their time in college with faith intact. It's a common trend, though not what one would expect at an institution explicitly steeped in faith. What helped me hold on was the Eucharist, taking it in as often as I could, staying with it regardless of what I felt, eating the body of Christ again and again so that Christ was within me. Even if I didn't feel him close, he was close. Even if I couldn't believe in him at times, I could at least taste him.

"Lord, I believe; help my unbelief." Dr. Benson, one of my philosophy professors, said that this is one of the most important statements of faith a person can make. It is a statement of hope for belief and simultaneously an admission of doubt. We cannot always feel our faith. We cannot always know it. We cannot always possess it. These are, after all, the wrong hopes. That is why we need a body to hold on to. That is why we need a God we can eat—to remind us of the real object of our hunger. And so against the gluttony, against the life of smoke and cigarettes and the casual desires that were tearing me apart, I ate the bread, the flesh, the body.

Still I felt a hunger. I had no metabolism for the holy yet. I was like a new dieter left hungry by the first nourishing foods eaten in years.

14 Weeks to Ironman

7:00 a.m.
Lincoln Park, Chicago, Illinois

The city radiates heat even early, the asphalt mixing with exhaust, industry, and the humid July air. My body feels slow, my feet heavy, which could be explained by the heat, the five hours of sleep I got, or my slight hangover from a too-good night out with friends. I'm in Chicago for a conference, my days filled with workshops, and this is my only chance to work out today so I take it. I have to be here, heavy on the pavement, because if there is any bit of conventional triathlon wisdom I believe, it is the mantra "Never miss a workout." Leave it up to a decision, let a vacation throw me off, and I will suffer for it during the 140.6 miles of the Ironman. The marketers—those poets of the people—got it right: Just do it.

I head east under the "L" train tracks, past row houses and apartments, and then to the Lincoln Park Zoo. Running gets easier as I move. My body accepts my will and keeps on going. I think about the movie *Kekexeli: Mountain Patrol*. It is the story of a group of Tibetan men who committed their lives to protecting a rare and endangered antelope from poachers, whose hunts threatened to cause the antelopes' extinction. The men live in a rugged landscape, enduring cold, sleeplessness, and exhaustion—all to protect an animal. I wonder if I would have the willpower to do something so good, and I realize just how soft I really am.

I am a person from a culture that lacks grit, one that builds everything with a bent toward convenience. The "air-conditioned nightmare," Henry Miller once called American culture. Few of us know how to suffer even slightly for a greater good. When the going gets tough...we stop. Yet it is grit that we need, now more than ever. As Americans face everything from the obesity crisis to our ecological disasters, grit is the virtue that can help us to make hard, sacrificial choices: to bike rather than drive, to pass over refined and sugar-laden products in favor of foods grown closer to the earth. We need to learn how to work through suffering for the sake of something better and greater. There should be no roads to mountaintops, only trails.

But where do we learn grit in a world where convenience is king? Where we outsource all of the unpleasant realities of life to people and places we don't see—our clothes made in the hard labor of sweatshops, our trash magically disappeared to somewhere else? Where we drive climate-controlled cars to sit-down jobs where we work, surf the Internet, and eat foods designed to be eaten at car consoles rather than tables?

Some of us run, bike, and swim. We go for distance because we want to learn that deeply human virtue of grit. We want to be people who endure, and we want to feel the hard pleasure of enduring. There are other things to learn from running a 5K, which is over in less than half an hour. But you don't run a marathon, you don't run thirty-one or fifty miles on a trail, you don't push through the 140.6 miles of an Ironman, without grit. Just watch the Ironman World Championship;

some of the fittest people in the world suffer, fall, and collapse. These are athletes who do nothing but train for this event, yet not every racer makes it to the end. In a 5K, most everyone finishes.

Just past the Lincoln Park Zoo, I follow the path through an underpass that goes beneath Lake Shore Drive, other runners funneling toward the lake from the Chicago streets. A long pedestrian path winds along Lake Michigan. Just below that is one of the city's sandy beachfronts. Cyclists whir past on the path, most of them on triathlon bikes. It's always the triathletes who are out; other cyclists train, but few are as consistent. It's not the road bikes that are out in the morning, even when people are on vacation. It's triathletes who whiz by at 6:00 a.m., never missing a workout, while their families sleep in condos nearby.

I go down to one of the long piers that reach out into the lake. I take off my shoes and socks, my sunglasses and hat, then strip down to the competition-style jammer swimsuit I am wearing beneath my running shorts. The water is clear and cold, wild and open. The city cannot enter it. The shore is the boundary against the concrete and glass of the city; the lake meets any attempt at encroachment with erosion, a storm, wild movements of its waters.

Most swims these days take place in a pool. *Twenty-five meters, turn…twenty-five meters, turn.* In a pool there is none of the feel of the open water, vast and dangerous, in which I will be swimming my 2.4 miles come fall. There are no big waves in a pool.

The water is fresh here in Lake Michigan. But there is something about the horizon that spreads on and on across the lake that makes it resemble the ocean more closely than any pool could. This morning gives me a taste of what the swim will be like in November, each stroke pushing against that endless watery edge, vast and unpredictable.

I wade in, breathe deep, and spread my body across the water's surface.

This Is My
Body in the Zoo

My first job out of college that offered a paycheck and insurance and an ID badge with a lanyard was at the Cudahy Library of Loyola University in Chicago. I lived in Rogers Park, a short walk from campus on the north side of the city, just off the Loyola stop. I shared an apartment with Alex, a friend from Wheaton who was now in the economics PhD program at Northwestern.

It was my routine to wake up early, walk to the library before it was open, work for an hour on the short stories I was learning to write, and then begin my eight-hour workday of book processing and web surfing. The work was sometimes interesting, but there was never enough to do. It was a job that required a college degree and entailed a forty-hour workweek, but it would have been a better fit for a part-time student worker. I would beg for more work, but after a few hours of actually doing my job each day I spent the rest of my time listening to podcasts, reading websites, and learning about anything that appealed to me—from the history of the Arab-Zionist conflict to the latest underground hip-hop group.

At that job I experienced my first cubicle, my first desk, and my first "ergonomic" office chair, all placed in a back corner of a large, windowless room where several boxes of library books arrived each day to be checked, labeled, and sent out to the shelves. College life had been active by comparison: walking from class to class, walking from the cafeteria to the library, walking with friends to the train, walking to coffee shops and study spots. I never sat for more than a couple of hours. Now, I was mostly sitting for two four-hour stretches each day, my body illumined not by the sun but by fluorescents flickering overhead and the blue light of LCD screens before me.

The only time I got outside was during smoke breaks and lunch hour. With the staff being made up of mostly grad students and would-be grad students, there were plenty of people taking smoke breaks. This became a kind of regular social outlet for us on the library's loading dock. Tom the Mail Guy talked to us about his various left-leaning conspiracies. These being the days just after the attacks of 9/11 and before the Iraq War, he had plenty.

In those days smoking helped me make friends—a cigarette or a light bummed, a conversation shared over the six minutes it took to reach the filter. Smoking was also an excuse to step away from the desk and go outside. Whether there was cold, rain, or burning days of August sun, it didn't matter; six minutes, a few times a day, gave me relief and provided space for something healthy (a mental break, fresh air) at the same time it was taking my health away.

I suppose I could have taken a short walk during those times, but there was no small gathering of walkers. There was no compulsion to gather every couple of hours for a lakeside stroll. And cigarettes are a great cure for the stress found in cubicle life. I would get anxious about a girl, graduate school applications, or any of the things that can come up in the life of a twenty-two-year-old who suddenly finds himself in the real world of jobs and relationships and money. A short smoke would set it all at ease—a nicotine fix for anxiety.

Sometimes during my lunch hour I'd try to get healthy, or at least look healthy. I had free access to the campus fitness center, so I would go down and do a haphazard circuit of the strength machines. It was a gym where graying faculty members worked on their blood pressure alongside students, mostly men, who were attempting to perfect every minor muscle of their bodies in preparation for spring break on Panama City's beaches.

On alternate days I used the cardio machine, whittling away for half an hour at the regular Coke I'd drunk at lunch. The "calories burned" numbers slowly rose as I watched the TV news, the daytime soaps, the sports that blared from above. Once in a while I played racquetball with a fellow library worker who was slowly finishing a PhD in philosophy.

My lungs heaved with the effort of exercise, and so I occasionally tried to stop smoking. This never lasted long—a week at most. As a twenty-something in Chicago it seemed to me as though everyone smoked. I figured that between that and the constant brown haze of summer air pollution, I might as well get some pleasure from the dissolution of my pulmonary system. A person could just as well get cancer from the sun, I reasoned. "Life," I wrote at one point in my notebook, "seems a carcinogen."

I was lonely without family close by or the ready friendships of college. Going out, having dinner, going for a walk, and meeting someone new all took work and risks that I hadn't needed to take in all my years in school, where such things came easy. A few of my college friends were still around in the city. But I longed for something more. I longed for a girl I could share my life with. And as has always been the case when I had no prospects of romance and no girl on my arm, I began to worry about my body.

Since exercise wasn't getting me far I decided to change what I could: my wardrobe. I'm not a clothes kind of person. I have a couple of basic outfits that I just rotate endlessly. But being in the city with a real job, surrounded by style, I decided I needed a new look. Matt, a friend from college and recent employee-of-the-month at Express, said he could help.

I get overwhelmed in stores like Express and generally I want nothing to do with the employees, who are always offering clothes I know won't fit right. But I was here to shop with Matt, and he took an almost tender approach to helping me. I bought gray and khaki pants, black-striped shirts, and a brown pea coat that I still wear over a decade later, the ends of the sleeves only now beginning to fray. It was the best wardrobe I've ever had. I signed the agreement for an Express card. I became a consumer in a way I'd never been before.

With my new urban wardrobe I got compliments, and this gave me the confidence to talk to girls I had previously admired only from afar. I felt cool in my Euro-style shoes and gray pants that somehow made my butt look good as I stood there, a cigarette in my hand. Buying became, in that first steady flow of money into my life, another kind of compulsion. The solution to a bad day became a new book, a new CD—each purchase setting a flow of serotonin rippling over the little pleasure sensors in my brain. This was a new kind of gluttony—a million little pleasures distracting from the deeper pleasure that comes from experiencing limits and "noes."

Pleasure needs patience. No fast-food meal ever won a James Beard Award, and it would be a waste anyway to eat such a fine meal while on the road. But we rarely have the patience to wait for the deepest pleasures of life. Whether this is a particular problem of our age or if it comes from some disquiet long found in the human self, few of us want to wait to feel good. More than that, we want any discomfort—any suffering, psychological or otherwise—to end immediately. So we smoke and eat and shop and participate in all the small satisfactions that never seem to add up to a whole, while that whole keeps looming over us as if taunting us in our inability to reach it.

I began to look around at the cubicle life I'd entered, the mechanical life of train schedules and buses. The only mitigation of the seeming absurdity was a good bottle of Scotch and a pack of cigarettes, or momentary lust over a girl working behind a counter. I began to feel like I was inside a cage, like we all were—pacing around in our imitation habitats, not realizing there was something more beyond our walls.

Perhaps as long as the modern world has been around, there has also existed the idea that somewhere else in our past or in some far-flung corner of the world there exists some natural, simpler, and more authentic way of living. The grass is always greener, so they say, but at least where it is green there is grass. The ideal of a truly natural way of living might be just an ideal, but it persists, I think, because it names a longing we all have for a pure human life, a shared nostalgia for Eden.

The reality is that our lives today are deeply disconnected from our biology and our fundamental nature. The countryside isn't pure, but cities and suburbs go one step further, insulating us from the natural limits and reality of ourselves. When we live in environments designed to cater to human desires, it can be hard to see any other reality. Our cars allow us to think that we can go fast without consequences; our systems of waste disposal and sewage convince us that we need not care about our trash. With the flush of the toilet we spirit away what some other cultures see as a gift for the garden—disrupting the essential cycle that retained nutrients in each place. Food comes packaged and prepared; animals are delivered bloodless and shrink-wrapped—"protein products," the agribusiness industry calls them.

Erwan Le Corre is a fitness coach and founder of a workout program that directs participants to climb trees, crawl through bushes, and "move naturally." Le Corre calls contemporary society "life in the zoo." We are, he says, like caged animals fed artificial diets in artificial environments—lazy lions who have forgotten how to hunt. In videos posted online, the Frenchman runs shirtless and barefoot through the forest, scrambling up trees, his lean, muscled body moving in ways he imagines to be primitive; he works to shape his body in the ways he believes consistent with the ways humans have exercised throughout most of our time on this planet. Danger and romanticism can be found in this longing for an authentic, natural self, but so can truth.

There is no denying that bodies have become something other than what they were designed for, that the very context in which we try to achieve health is flawed. "The zoo" is an apt description. We live in synthesized and unnatural environments; we eat synthesized and unnatural foods. Today, barefoot running, the Paleo diet and lifestyle, natural foods, primitivism, and a whole host of other movements aim to direct us toward a life that conforms better to our biology, our ecology, our purpose. As the city wore on my spirit and body, I tried to get back to something of this "natural" self.

Around the corner and down a block from my apartment I found a small organic grocery store. It had bulk items for sale, a small freezer of meat, a mix of produce and dry goods. It was the kind of old-fashioned store that let customers keep an account tallied on a sheet of paper kept behind the counter. One of its primary sources of revenue was a weekly produce box, full of a variety of fresh organic vegetables grown on farms from around the Chicago area. My roommate and I became subscribers.

Every week we picked up our big box of organic vegetables, a friendly newsletter tucked inside with a list of the vegetables for that week. We were both fairly ignorant about the food, and every week offered a new discovery. Bok choy, kohlrabi, daikon radish—even kale was unknown to me. As I sorted through the box I would have to guess at what was what. Then came the question of what to do with it all. I would go online and look for recipes ingredient by ingredient. It was an ignorant way to cook—buying all we needed for each recipe rather than being creative with what we already had—but it was how I learned. After a few months I became a passable cook.

I was drawn to organic produce in part for health reasons but also because I was concerned about the ecological problem of pesticides. I'd been an environmentalist from a young age; my first major school paper in ninth grade was a review of Rachel Carson's book *Silent Spring*, a classic of the environmental movement that led to the ban of the pesticide DDT. But much of my environmentalism had been of the preservationist brand. I was against pollution and clear cutting because I was *for* the saving of endangered species and endangered places. Yet I had not become conscious of the links between my food, my health, and the health of the planet.

In those produce boxes I discovered the truth that what was good for my body was good for the earth and vice versa. My guide in this development of my thinking was Wendell Berry, the poet-prophet, farmer-writer of Kentucky. I'd begun reading some of Berry's essays in college. Then at Loyola I found a clothbound copy of *The Unsettling of America* in the library's discard pile.

His essay "The Body and the Earth," which I found in that book, named exactly the kind of fundamental disconnect I was feeling within myself. Berry explains that the very idea of health is connected, in its root and etymology, to the idea of wholeness.

> It is therefore absurd to approach the subject of health piecemeal
> with a departmentalized band of specialists. A medical doctor
> uninterested in nutrition, in agriculture, in the wholesomeness

of mind and spirit is as absurd as a farmer who is uninterested in health. Our fragmentation of this subject cannot be our cure, because it is our disease. The body cannot be whole alone. Persons cannot be whole alone. It is wrong to think that bodily health is compatible with spiritual confusion or cultural disorder, or with polluted air and water or impoverished soil.[17]

This was my life that Berry was describing: divided and disconnected. I ate good food then smoked a cigarette afterward. I exercised to balance out the calorie intake of my lunchtime soda and morning doughnut. I prayed and took Eucharist weekly at the Episcopal church a few blocks north of my apartment, but then lived as though faith and Jesus and holiness didn't matter. With Berry's help I began to see that I would not quit smoking, would not put aside my loneliness, would not live the kind of integrated life that hums with real harmony until I changed something more fundamental about myself. I needed to inhabit the world in a different way than I had been doing. I had to change the way my body was present in the world.

"To try to heal the body alone is to collaborate in the destruction of the body. Healing is impossible in loneliness; it is the opposite of loneliness. Conviviality is healing. To be healed we must come with all the other creatures to the feast of Creation," Berry wrote in "The Body and the Earth."[18] It was around those first meals—cooking vegetables, carefully saving the scraps to drop in the compost pile down the street at the Waldorf School garden—that I began to escape some of my loneliness. Our friend Jaime came to dinner every Thursday night, and often other guests came too. We ate together, learning the arts of conviviality and finding that the good and healthy life is a life enjoyed in togetherness.

Cooking became a nexus, a physical act in which disconnected pieces of my life gathered together and became more cohesive. There was the earth from which the vegetables came, that grew the green grass that fed cattle whose beef we would eat. There was the meal: a feast we would share. There was my body, which took in the food and digested and reorganized its proteins and amino acids, its carbs and fats, into my skin and bones and fat and flesh. And though I didn't say it publicly enough at that time, there was the blessing, which acknowledged that the meal we were eating—the gifts of the land and rain and work—was also a transcendent gift that went beyond any attempt to reduce food to mere commodity that can be bought and sold.

And yet even in the healing environment of this conviviality, I began to feel like the pace of urban life—an eight-hour workday spent twiddling time away before a blue screen—was out of pace with the rhythm of a truly human life. In "The Body and the Earth," Berry wrote, "Past the scale of the human, our works do not liberate us—they confine us. They cut off access to the wilderness of Creation where we must go to be reborn."[19] I felt that. I felt trapped by my work, by the metal and concrete of the city, and I longed to be reborn.

I wanted out of the zoo. I wanted to live in a way that was connected to the "wilderness of Creation," where my body would make sense. I wanted my health to be the natural result of good work and good eating. More and more I wanted to follow Berry's example, to return to the countryside and put my body in a place where health in all of its wholeness could come to me. I was convinced that the city was my problem, that my body, my spirit, my soul could never thrive there. I began to plan my escape.

I had one lead: a farmer in Arkansas who raised sheep, kept honeybees, and was a leader in the sustainable agriculture movement. He lived and farmed on a small bit of acreage near where I'd gone to high school, and his daughter and I had been friends. He agreed to let me come and learn from him how to farm. I would work a few days a week, learning the chores. Slowly, as I became more helpful, I would earn things in barter: sheep of my own, farm equipment.

I found a job in Arkansas teaching part-time, and my parents, glad at the prospect of having their son back home, said I could live with them while I saved for a place of my own. So midway through that summer—right when Chicago is so alive, soaking in the few days of sunshine before the long winter—I made my escape from the zoo. No more cubicles or office chairs or long hours spent before a blue screen, wondering what to do while the required minutes clicked by. From now on my work would also be my exercise; I would eat food that I raised, and I would live in harmony with the creation from which I would draw my health.

That October the blue Arkansas sky seemed to spread forever overhead; the sky was scraped by cumulus clouds and hawks swirling beneath making their way south. Meadowlarks sang long trills from the grass while sheep, calm and silent, grazed the fading green of the field. This was creation, good and healthy, the kind of place where my body could find wholeness and peace.

I sat on a log, crooked and bleached white. After reaching inside my shirt pocket, I pulled out a pack of Camels and lit a cigarette, deeply inhaling the blue-gray smoke.

Let animals out of a cage and most will come back.

12 Weeks to Ironman

5:30 p.m.
Allsopp Park, Little Rock, Arkansas

Where the sidewalk meets the wide brick plaza, a wide concrete staircase descends down a hill to a rocky, root-filled trail. This is my exit; the place where I leave the world of cars and exhaust, deadlines and computers, all the demands and rush of urban life. The trail twists and undulates along ridgelines and around creek beds. The steep hillsides kept this forest free from development when this neighborhood was settled in the late nineteenth century. Now they are a reminder of wildness in the middle of the city, a place where deer and foxes and coyotes are seen less than a mile from the glass and steel skyline of corporate campuses.

When I run, I like to run here, chickadees scolding from the oaks and hickories that insulate this quiet place from the noise of nearby streets. It's a mile of concrete sidewalk to the park. My legs adjust to the rhythm of the run, my pace unnatural on the pavement. But after those stairs my body enters a primal space. It feels good to run, to breathe hard, to sweat. It feels like my body is meant for running in the woods.

A friend of mine recently took up running. After a few weeks she was having some foot pain, so she went to a podiatrist. He told her to quit running, to buy bulky orthotics, and to stick to cycling. "Our bodies," he told her, "weren't meant for running."

That's a common line, but the evidence tips to the contrary. In the animal kingdom, human beings may be uniquely good at running. Not the sprints of gazelle and cheetahs, but long runs in the arid heat. Our relative hairlessness, our sweat, and the form of our feet all point to bodies designed for running long distances. Given enough miles, a fit human can beat just about any animal in a foot race. The famous one-hundred-mile Western States Endurance Run began as a horse race. Then people started running it, and some even beat the horses by hours. That famous quote from *Chariots of Fire,* when Eric Liddell says, "I believe God made me for a purpose... And when I run I feel His pleasure,"[20] reflects the idea that when we run we are living into the bodies for which we were created.

My body is pouring sweat thirty minutes in; even with its quick-wicking, breathable fabric my shirt is soaked. I take it off, letting the sweat do its work of evaporative cooling. I wouldn't do this on the road; I'm still too uncertain of my body, too hesitant about the stubborn jiggle of my midline. But on these trails, alone in the woods, I like to run shirtless, feeling animal-like and alive.

My body moves in wild, natural rhythms, and I try to let the wisdom of my body come through. Good running coaches often say: "If you want to see good form, watch a child." Bad form is caused by the contortion of our natural gait by overly corrective shoes. It can take years to train our feet out of the bad habits caused by thick soles. Just as Michelangelo's *David* once lay hidden in a block of marble, waiting for its form to be revealed, we all have the bodies we possess and the bodies that are yet to be revealed when the resurrection comes. While running those hillside trails, I feel in my muscles and tendons, and in the air against my skin, some hint of that resurrection body; I feel that I am meant for this.

Meant for this? At some point that's the question we must come to terms with about our bodies: Do they have a specific purpose—a shape into which they are meant to be formed? If we are not just the outcome of a random, long-ago collision of amino acids—if a mind was attached to hands that formed our bodies from the clay—then our forms hold an intention. Our bodies have purpose and meaning—but what? What are we to make of the shape of our flesh, so beautiful and fallible, so strong and weak?

The answers offered to us are a schizoid array from across the spectrum of American culture. Doctors tell us we are getting sick and fat; cholesterol and blood pressure are on the rise, and statins and blood thinners are available at every pharmacy. Dietitians and preventive care are available to help us preserve the bodies we'll continue to need if we're to survive long enough to live in a nursing home. The body's wholeness and health are now defined by those exams and tests that are covered by an insurance plan.

Go to a grocery store magazine rack and you'll get more answers. *Popular Science* has a cover story about the scientific quest to engineer the perfect athlete. *Fitness* promises the key to "Find Your Inner Winner, Strategies for a Braver Bolder You." *Cosmopolitan* has the "Bikini Body Plan." *Men's Health* recirculates the evergreen offer to help readers "Get Back in Shape," promising "Results in Two Weeks!" *Maxim*, claiming to represent "what guys want," asks the enticing question "Does Beer Make Us Stronger?"

The glossies seem to concur: a lack of six-pack abs condemns people to being the last who will find fulfillment in the flesh. Meanwhile, food manufacturers wait in the wings, alternately tempting consumers and promising free passes, such as low-fat cookies and guilt-free ice cream. Our churches tell us that the fat are gluttons, the beautiful are temptations, and our bodies are the shells we will one day shed for heaven.

None of those answers to the meaning and purpose of my flesh seems adequate to my body as I run down this trail in the Arkansas woods. I have never understood the idea of a God who would create a good world, take on flesh to save it, and then burn it all up so that he can send a limited number of his many creatures to a heaven that exists only on some other spiritual realm. Then again, the idea that we are simply bodies has never fit with the fullness of my experience. What is the part of me that is overwhelmed at the beach by the vastness of the horizon? Soul? Spirit? It is something beyond skin.

The problem with all these attempts at explaining the human shape—offered in a range of places, from magazines to pulpits—is that none of them get at the whole of the person, the complex and contextual reality of human life. Questions of shape are better answered by the idea that each person's shape, now and to come, is more like a puzzle piece than it is like the completed puzzle; each shape fits with other shapes to form a greater whole. We are individuals, yes, but we are also members of ecosystems, economies, communities.

There can be no healthy body without healthy work, there can be no healthy sex without healthy love, and there can be no well-being of heart and mind outside the well-being of the ecology surrounding each human life. We can't get our bodies into shape without also getting our souls and minds and ecosystems into shape. Eat and exercise all you want, but if you live in a place and world that is toxic, the most you can hope for is better protection. The riboflavin in fresh vegetables, when consumed, may help offset the presence of carcinogenic toxins at the industrial site down the road, but they won't change fact that the threat of cancer lurks in our unraveling ecosystems.

That the contours of a healthy body mean not only health alone but health that fits into a whole makes sense only if we see our bodies as reflections of God's body. *Imago Dei,* the image of God, is an idea taken from Genesis where God states that man is made in "our image." This *our,* plural, reflects in the Christian interpretation the idea that God is not a lonely singularity but a community of three—a Trinity engaged in a constant dance of love, each member of the three moving in perfect, harmonic response to the others. If the human shape reflects God's shape, then we must view the healthy shape of human beings as a communion and community, with God, with each other, and with the whole of creation born from the love of God.

Alone in the woods, I am not alone. As I run, I release my created body into the creation of which it is a part. For this moment I am free from competing definitions of my self, free from the mirrored walls found in chain gyms, free from my own envious glances at the guy-with-the-chiseled-abs running past, free from the persistent temptation to think this body won't matter in the long-run anyway.

The trail twists around, over a bridge and up a steep climb, ending at a neighborhood street. Then it's back to cars and crowds and the hard surface of concrete. I put on my shirt at the forest's edge. The animal-like aliveness I felt begins to fade. Now it's just the hard effort to finish out the run, pushing along the sidewalk that leads home. In that hour in the woods I have renewed myself. I have known for a moment what it is to return to the shape—physical, spiritual, whole—for which I was meant.

This Is My
Body on the Farm

In the headlights' glow I can see the eager faces of the sows, their breath leaving small clouds in the cold. The sun is still east, somewhere over the Atlantic by now. I climb out of the cab and drop the gate of the truck. In the back is a fifty-pound bag of corn, its brown paper marked with a camo pattern. This is supplement feed for the pigs, to add to the acorns and tubers and other food they forage in the large area of oak and pine where they roam freely throughout the day. They squeal and snort with excitement as I walk to the feeder and dump the bag in the top. Their water has a thin layer of ice over it, which I break with a hammer. The temperatures will rise; the ice won't refreeze today.

I check on the sheep, moving them to a new paddock of pasture bordered by portable fences that I set up the day before. Burley, the white Great Pyrenees sheepdog, greets me, and I feed him too, in a bowl he fiercely guards from sheep that hover, hoping to steal the meal. This dog stays with the sheep and was raised with them as a puppy. I try not to be too friendly. He has a job: to live here in the pasture and act as alpha predator. In the world of nature, one old rancher once told me, "The sheep guard dog is regarded by the other predators as the biggest, baddest coyote on the block." Most coyotes would stay away from this dog; he's twice their size. But recently a few have been coming around. I've found two dead lambs and a ewe in the past week, blood and entrails spilled across the grass. This morning, mercifully, there have been no kills.

For the sheep I have a bale of alfalfa hay, their winter supplement until the green grass of spring sprouts up again. I cut the twine binding the bales at the knot, wrapping it in loops and leaving it by the barn on a nail. Twine is a useful tool for future projects such as fixing broken fences; it's the duct tape of farm life.

I break the ice in the trough for the cattle, big and black and yet so gentle in their shadowy predawn silhouettes. I feed and water the chickens, letting the laying hens out of their nighttime roosts inside the coop. I test the electric fence and check on the ewe in the barn, a little old and sick, not handling her current pregnancy so well. I shut the gate. Ahead of me are a dirt road, highway, shower, and a one-hour drive down to Little Rock where I will spend the day teaching high school before returning to check on the animals again and prepare for the next day's farmers' market. Rinse and repeat. That was how my days went in my first years of farming.

I had graduated from being Al's apprentice to being a small-scale farmer in my own right. It started with the pigs that I had acquired through a deal with one of Al's friends in Tennessee. Then I started managing some sheep for Al, a flock of ewes that had long lived on the pasture I leased from him. I added cattle as well, a few Angus-cross calves I grazed for beef. Next came chickens: laying hens and meat birds. I sold the meat and eggs from the farm at the farmers' market and to chefs at the better restaurants in Little Rock. This was what I had dreamed of while sitting on the lakeshore in Chicago, imagining pure life in the country. Much of that promise had been fulfilled.

My farm life was formed as much by my neighbors as it was by the animals. These were the farmers and country folk who called each other if a cow got out or if help was needed to put up a load of hay before rain came. These included characters like Danny, a red-headed country boy who drove a big Dodge Ram and once showed me the small arsenal he kept in his basement. Meri, short for "America," lived off the garden she kept and the deer she and her husband shot each season. Denis was an Amish Mennonite farmer to whom I sold pigs and on whose behalf I bootlegged raw milk. Finally there was Al: brilliant, troubled, made haggard by debt. Al seemed never to sleep; he was ready to help and was extremely generous at times, but he seemed reckless at other times. He taught me much, but his temper drove me to find my distance soon. He could be as manipulative as he was kind.

My memories of that first winter I spent with the animals are marked by smells and tastes. I remember the way my hands felt while grasping hard at the loose flank of a ewe that spring; I held her caught between my legs so I could give her wormer before the parasites emerged in the grass. There was the feel of blood, warm and thick, red with oxygen, that pumped from the slit throat of a lamb that would be dinner. There was the sharp prick of alfalfa; the burn of the string and wires of the bale against my hands as I lifted it onto the truck. There was the soft lanolin of lamb's wool, a natural lotion that softened my calluses. There was the long wooden handle of the pitchfork I used to dig into the compost pile, where I buried the lambs that didn't make it—the nitrogen of their bodies mixing with the carbon of the wood, transformed by heat to black soil with a few bone fragments mixed in, over three months' time.

In my years of farming, my hands changed more than any other part of my body. They became rough with calluses that spread across my palms. Five years' worth of books and computer keyboards hadn't left a single mark on my hands. And even though I had always used my hands, even while pursuing the most abstract of knowledge work—my hands turning pages, my fingers playing across the QWERTY arrangement of letters on the keyboard—I had never been forced to be as conscious of them as I was in those fields: my fingers with their multitude of joints and bones, my palms strong with muscle, connecting the intentions of my mind with the actions of my body in a world of grass and animals and dirt.

Hands are the point at which human minds meet the world; they are the formational extension of our brains. Full of nerve endings, hands can manipulate and feel in a way that's unique in nature. The phrase "hands-on learning" is redundant because our deepest learning is always hands-on. Gestures of the hands are our first language—a caress, our most intimate expression of love; a strike, our most dangerous show of anger. Both are rooted in our hands.

Artists have long recognized the importance of the hand. Rodin, the sculptor most famous for *The Thinker,* was obsessed with hands. I once saw an exhibit featuring a whole series of his hand sculptures —small and large, powerful, slender—all of them extended in gestures that made it easy to imagine a body lurking invisibly behind them. *The Thinker,* a material reflection on the immaterial stuff of thought, captures that act through its image of a huge hand folded beneath the chin. It is no wonder that when painting the Sistine Chapel, Michelangelo wanted to portray the connection between the divine and the human, and he did so using the muscled hand of God reaching toward the outstretched fingers of Adam.

As I became aware of my hands in my work, I became aware of other experiences from which I'd also been disconnected—perceptions shut off by shoes and clothes. What would it be like to feel at any moment the cool and wet of the earth, the dry crackle of grass, the dampness of last fall's leaves? Our bodies were made to sense the world—to not only see and hear, but to touch and feel the creation on us and with us and around us. It's as though, with the shame of Adam and Eve after the Fall, we covered our skin and disconnected our bodies from the world, cutting ourselves off from all God made.

I had started farming because I felt deeply the loss that came with the Fall, and I hoped that if I lived and worked in creation, then perhaps I would begin to reconnect those severed ties. But the problem of a disconnected life can't be solved through a change of location, as rich as some new context might be. My days of farming were instructive, but I was left with lessons half learned—fast-sprouting seeds without good soil to receive them. My farming life sprang up brilliant and green, but after a few short years it began to wither as its shallow roots dried up.

There were days when I would make a big sale and deposit a quarter of a year's salary in the bank; just as quickly the tractor would break, feed costs would rise, and my old truck would suddenly die. Credit card swipe. I was exuberant in the face of possibility and let my ambition outstrip my skills. I moved too quickly to try to make my living from the land, not letting the land teach me how to do it. Though I worked with my neighbors I was mostly alone in my work, and I had taken on more work than I could handle. I added chickens before I had mastered pigs. I expanded my flock to five hundred before I had successfully husbanded a fifth of that. My meager earnings from teaching part-time kept me afloat, but with increasing frequency I deposited those magic checks offered by credit-card companies, to tide me over until my next big payday.

I could sell products easily enough. A hundred chickens? Sure! Then I was up all night trying to process them. I spent more time in the truck than I did in the pasture. I drove to the farm. I drove the hour to market. I drove the two and a half hours to the slaughterhouse. I made the rounds of the high-end restaurants to which I sold. NPR, Red Bull, and cigarettes carried me along—my mind always amped and buzzing about the news of the day; my lungs always slightly aching.

At day's end when no more driving could be done, the sun set long before, I felt too tired to cook the good food I grew. I got takeout: Chinese buffet, gas-station pizza, loaded nachos. I answered the call of my loneliness with marathon episodes of *Lost,* smoke breaks taken in between episodes to distract me from myself. I was too tired and busy to question the reality I was living. I had come to the farm to live a Sabbath life in balance with the economies and rhythms of nature; instead I was living against all that, without the community or the health for which I had hoped.

I have a photo of myself that was taken at the beginning of my farming days. In it I'm wearing a plaid shirt, twin lambs in my arms, my face smiling. A similar picture was taken three years later. I am holding a chicken, a plaid shirt still my style, my smile broad and ready as always. But in that photo my face has changed; it is puffy and broad, lipids accumulated in my cheeks.

I began my farming work a little high on the BMI (body mass index), but I was not obese. I was a steady 180 pounds; not skinny, but the number fit my mesomorph, five-foot, nine-inch frame just fine. At the end of my farming days I weighed over 250, my pants size at the upper limits of what I could find at Walmart. Despite all my hopes for health, I had become a part of that statistical climb toward obesity that has marked public conversation. I had wanted to find an answer, a kind of wholeness; instead I found myself just another number in the trend.

My body had become an echo of my spirit. I read theology and even wrote (through grace, more than through my own understanding) some reflections about farming and faith that felt true. But inside I drew a blank. I was uneasy about this but seemed unable to turn my desire toward God or any real good. I went to church out of duty more than for any other reason. Without an Episcopal option nearby, I attended a Presbyterian church for a while. But its Sundays were made of staid sermons and mostly empty pews, and I quit soon enough.

I wanted the connection found in a long conversation, but God seemed an omnipresent absence. I felt angry that my farming life was falling apart, angry at my body and my inability to eat what I should eat, angry that I could not stop smoking. Most of all I was angry that I hadn't found a love who would embrace my body and stay with it, whether it was sick or healthy. I blamed God: all-powerful, all-beneficent Creator of us all. What reward had I received for my belief? Could God not fill my empty life with happiness?

I felt an affinity for Cain, the brother who went to work in the fields and tried to make a living in post-Eden life by growing vegetables amid rocks and thorns. What did he get for his work, his offering? A God who needed nothing rejected everything Cain had to give. What more did God want than the best of his work? Or mine? My life felt futile. I was tired of trying to be good. I was tired of God and of all my attempts to please God. Tired of all of the inadequate churches and inadequate Christians. I wanted a vacation from God and from the moral life I felt was interrupting my happiness.

Bon voyage! I left God on the beach of my imagination. I knew that God existed somewhere and was not a figment of my thoughts, but I was no longer willing to organize my life around God's presence. This departure had happened as most spiritual departures do, before I realized I was on the journey. But now, seeing God in the distance, I was ready to turn toward some other horizon. I was sure I'd come back someday after I had found my happiness and could allow God to enter into my joy.

So, obese and disappointed, debt-ridden and as lonely as I'd ever been, I began to look elsewhere for solutions to my unraveling life and my disordered body. I wanted acceptance and relief; I wanted happiness in the midst of my sorrow. And so I looked to the best God-replacements anyone has ever found: sex and love, just the things about which "God," that jealous sacrificer of my joy, had already been making me feel guilty.

10 Weeks to Ironman

10 a.m., Saturday morning
CrossFit Little Rock

I reach down into the chalk bucket, my hands sweaty and slick in the Arkansas humidity and heat. High-capacity warehouse fans whir in the open doors, but this doesn't help much. The flow is more like the air in a convection oven than it is a cool reprieve.

I turn to the bar lying on the ground in front of me: forty-five pounds of iron with two big twenty-five-pound, rubber-padded plates stacked on the ends. I remember what Coach Lambert has told me: *Back flat; chest out; arms wide.* I pull up slowly at first, keeping my knees and shoulders aligned, not letting my butt come up too fast. Then I pull quickly and thrust my hips forward, pushing the bar up. As it rises I try to drop my body beneath it, finally catching it with my arms locked overhead—an act that's about agility as much as it is about strength.

"Nice snatch," Eric says. He's small framed and strong, but not overbuilt. His goal isn't to become some Jersey Shore hulk but to actually be strong and fit for whatever life might bring in his role as an Air Force pilot. Eric can snatch three times what I can; I don't take his compliment lightly. Eric has nearly perfect form. He studies Olympic lifting as a serious art and science. He knows what's behind his every muscle twitch and how much protein to take in after a workout. He has perfected his form through daily practice spent moving his body closer and closer to the ideal form for each lift. Watching him lift weights is like watching a great dancer perform a pirouette.

"It finally just felt right," I say.

"Teaching a lift is like teaching someone to paint," Eric says, turning to me from his own bar. "You can teach all of the form and techniques to someone, but if he's going to make art, something has to happen inside of him." Was I in a CrossFit gym trying to get ripped or in some yoga studio getting my chakras opened?

I'd come to CrossFit to prepare my body for the beating it would take at the triathlon coming up in November. CrossFit and its benefits are a controversial topic in the field of endurance sports and in the fitness world in general. A "trend," a "fad," a "masochistic waste of time that could be better spent biking, running, or swimming"—I knew all of the arguments against it. But from the moment I started doing the workouts posted online daily at CrossFit Endurance, I loved the soreness I felt in my body, the increasing muscle strength, the technical movements, the dedication to good form and nutrition—the attention to every detail of fitness.

When I started going to a CrossFit gym, I found a community of people who loved the kind of raw workout I wanted. There was none of the Nautilus-pushing, micro-muscle-perfecting strength training that's traditionally practiced by bodybuilders. The gym was located in a big warehouse filled with rubber mats and the smell of sweat, dubstep and hip-hop blasting on loudspeakers; rubber-coated iron plates stood in big stacks alongside pull-up bars and kettlebells. You will never see mirrors in a CrossFit gym. "In CrossFit the only mirror is your soul," some coaches say.

I hadn't expected people to talk about the soul when I first came to CrossFit. Lifting barbells, working out in short bursts so intensely that I felt I might vomit, leaving a workout with my hands and body trembling—that's what I expected to happen and all those things did. But what I also found was an understanding of the body and its movements that felt closer to the traditions of dance than of bodybuilding. CrossFitters have no use for movements like curls—an exercise that develops muscles few of us use in everyday life, its benefits cosmetic more than functional. CrossFit values strength and speed and form all in equal measure. The fitness it offers is of the generally prepared variety, rather than the specialized athletics common to those who can run a fast 800m but can't do twenty pull-ups.

Many people come to CrossFit for the group atmosphere, the camaraderie that comes from doing something hard together with others. It is competition in its oldest form—people striving together and pushing one another on. Something else that draws people to CrossFit is its emphasis not on looking fit but on *being* fit. Sure, there are photos of ripped CrossFit stars with six-pack abs, but with no mirrors in the gym you won't catch those people looking at themselves. Most people's experience of exercise comes from working out on strength machines in a company gym or running thirty mindless minutes on a treadmill. CrossFit is a stark and exhilarating change.

To do CrossFit right is to bring your entire self to it. To lift more weight from the floor than you've ever lifted. To keep perfecting the form of a lift until it finally clicks. To go faster and lift heavier than you did on the previous workout, in a way that requires everything of you. It is a workout that engages the whole of your body—your muscles and tendons and bones, as well as your brain.

It also requires the involvement of your spirit—that force within yourself that exists in and through your body but is not your body. It requires your heart; not just the pumping mass of blood that delivers oxygen to your tissues, but your heart that wants and has a will, that is somehow connected to your brain in a way that scientists are only now beginning to understand more fully, neurons present even in your pulsing chest.

It's time for a "Helen," a core CrossFit workout made up of a 400m run, twenty-one kettlebell swings, and twelve push-ups—all repeated three times, one after the other, as quickly as possible. The big timer on the wall is set to a three-two-one countdown. When the clock buzzes we dash out of the door toward the dumpster across the parking lot that marks the halfway point. Down and back. I try to keep my running form good: chest out, shoulders back, head upright and facing ahead. I try to pace myself. I want to go hard, but not so hard that I'll be unable to keep a good pace throughout the workout.

A couple of minutes later it's on to the kettlebell swings, an exercise done using a weight that looks like a cannonball with a handle—a fitness tool only the Russians could invent, crude yet effective. With both hands on the handle, my arms swing together as levers, and I use my hips to pop the ball up to eye level.

Next, it's the pull-up bars. I can't do twelve pull-ups in a row without stopping, not after the kettlebell swings. I jump up to the bar and try to finish in two sets of six. Then it's back out the door again for another run to the dumpster.

By the time the three rounds are finished I want to lie down, and I do—my body spread out on the rubber mat. Most of the others, as they finish, do the same.

"Good work, guys," says Lambert. "Be sure to stretch; do some foam rolling."

I get up, a little shaky. I gave it my all and there's a body-shaped sweat stain on the floor to prove it. Perhaps this is the most important thing I get from CrossFit: the psychological gift of knowing I can do something really hard, and the hard part will pass. This is a truth I will need to rely on in the race that looms ahead of me. It is a truth I first experienced the hard way, long before the Ironman.

This Is My Lonely Body

When I dreamed of the country life, I had imagined a pastoral world filled with hard work in the open air, good food at dinner, and a community that was close-knit and flourishing. I did find many of those things as I established my regular patterns. I ate breakfast at the Country Store gas station, where farmers gathered and drank coffee and ate biscuits smothered in chocolate gravy. At the feed store the dock guy, who helped me load chicken and pig feed into my truck, always joked, "Are you workin' hard or hardly workin'?" But even as I became a regular around town, my loneliness and isolation grew.

I had come back to a place where most people stayed and from which I had gone away. The people here knew the value of an acre and the prospects for soybeans. They knew where deer could be found and the best woods for hunting turkey. This was good and important knowledge, and the conversations that revolved around it were crucial, but these weren't the kind of conversations I'd been trained into. I wanted to talk independent film and philosophy; I wanted to talk about Dana Gioia's latest poetry collection and the urgency of the coming climate catastrophe. These weren't conversations I would find at the little Formica-topped tables in the Country Store.

What I couldn't find in the country I found in Little Rock among the local food and environmental activists who frequented the farmers' market. My stand was next to one belonging to Christian, a young, hipster farmer who dressed with an Arkansas twist on California cool. Earnest and hardworking, he grew salad greens and educated customers about the virtues of biodynamic farming while his two children, named after jazz singers, played among the vendors. On my other side was a large stand run by the Vangs, a Hmong family who had come to the United States as refugees from Southeast Asia. Mr. Vang was always smiling and joking with me, using gestures more than words. At the end of the day, he often gave me a load of beautiful Asian and standard vegetables to take home.

Just past the Vangs was a big stand run by Rusty and Sue Nuffer. The Nuffers may be the best farmers in Arkansas. They moved to the Ozarks during the back-to-the-land movement of the 1970s. But while most of those in the movement eventually returned to the northern cities from which they came, the Nuffers were among those who stayed and lived into their ideals. They cleared their land with mules and learned to grow organic vegetables better than anyone else in the Ozarks. The city's high-end chefs bought from them everything from deep violet carrots to rainbow varieties of potatoes—not the white russets used to make french fries, but the traditional Andean varieties of the Inca. Next to the Nuffers was Jody Hardin, a gregarious idea person from a long line of family farmers, now working hard to transition from his father's conventional farming ways to new organic practices. I often joined him and his crew at a pub after the market closed.

Customers ranged from the rector of the big downtown Episcopal parish to a local pot activist often seen circulating legalization petitions while obviously under the influence. The customers cared about what they bought and about the people from whom they bought it. They wanted the health that came from eating good food, and they wanted to support farming practices that were healthy for the land. Unfortunately, while I could talk honestly about the virtues of the meat I was offering—grass-fed, high in omega-3s, antibiotic-free—I did not model the truth of the food's goodness. I was selling a truth, but I wasn't living it.

One of my customers, Lorrie, was a personal trainer who bought pound upon pound of grass-fed meat and big jugs of the raw milk I was bootlegging for the Amish. I talked to her about fitness and healthy food. Many times she offered: "If you ever want a workout plan, I could help." I knew that I needed to do something different; I couldn't just keep buying new, larger pants and pack after pack of cigarettes.

In my first effort at doing *something* I bought a bike from Danielle, who ran a bike co-op near the market. I rode it up and down the country highway in front of my house in a halfhearted attempt at getting fit. But I had not been able to quit smoking—not with those long, lonely country nights of caffeine-fueled insomnia; not with all the hours I spent on the farm and working off-farm jobs in an attempt to hold my unraveling life together.

The best friendships I had in those days were formed through the Arkansas Sustainability Network. Around this time, I volunteered to help two of its founders, Katy and Danielle, in planning the Natural State Expo—a convention-style event that would showcase all of the ecological businesses and resources of Arkansas. There would be organic farmers, "green" building contractors, and electric-car enthusiasts alongside middle-school student presentations on sustainability: renewable energy, composting methods, pollution controls.

I worked with Danielle on media outreach. We contacted local television stations, and several of them, anxious to fill the minutes of those early morning shows, asked us to come and talk about the Expo.

A few days before our first interview, Danielle dropped out. Liz took her place.

I'd met Liz a few weeks before at a barbecue potluck at Danielle's apartment. It had been a gathering of hippie, environmentalist types who lived frugally and loved good food made from scratch—kimchi, pickles, beer and wine and mead. She was new to town, having taken a job with the Asia/South Pacific program of Heifer International, a sustainable development nonprofit agency. She had chestnut hair she kept back in a ponytail and wore glasses with thick, trendy rims over eyes that squinted when she smiled.

We decided to meet and talk about our morning show debut at Vino's, a dive that hosted both death-metal bands and hip-hop acts. It was the kind of place where rich and poor could come together around beer and pizza. Liz and I sat down with our planning notebooks, pizza, and pints. In between outlining Natural State Expo talking points, we talked about ourselves. I told her that I was a farmer, and that I wrote articles about food and sustainability for a handful of magazines. I learned that she had studied international relations, and had lived in Thailand and Australia and traveled throughout Asia with her work with Heifer. We enjoyed the conversation and the planning. When it came time to do our morning show interviews, we met before sunrise to drive to the TV studios together.

Under the guise of our continuing work on the media relations team for the Natural State Expo, we kept on meeting, spending more time learning about each other than we did planning media outreach. We looked for excuses to talk. Liz called me one night with a question about a mozzarella cheese recipe I'd given her. The question was frivolous and I knew that she was just making up an excuse to call. With that, I realized that the feelings that had been building in me were answered in her.

We held one of our last planning meetings on a restaurant balcony that overlooked the Arkansas River. We drank beer and talked, and in the warmth of the early fall sun, the tension of our unspoken feelings was palpable. Feelings of desire were strong for me, and I was with someone I wanted, who I could feel also wanted me. But I have always been cautious in love, never one to risk rejection.

We went to her office building with the excuse of her giving me an after-hours tour. As we stood beside her desk, looking out over the river through the big glass windows of one of Little Rock's first LEED-certified buildings, there was a moment of quiet when I felt as if I could kiss her. I hesitated to move toward her. But she felt it too because she turned to me and said, "I feel like there's a lot of chemistry between us, but I need to tell you that I'm kind of dating someone." She said it hesitantly, and I didn't know exactly what this meant for us, moving forward.

That night I made the hour drive back home from Little Rock along winding roads, the still light of the moon rippling through the trees, its sheen reflected on the lakes and ponds and streams I passed. I felt longing and loneliness, the combination I had experienced for too long. Longing and loneliness ate at me, and I was tired. I felt it in my heart, my muscles—an overwhelming disquiet and desperation.

Loneliness is powerful and dangerous, and it is not only a matter of the mind. Our bodies also become lonely. Psychologists who've studied children neglected in Romanian orphanages, and scientists who've worked with rhesus monkey infants separated from their mothers have documented the negative impact caused by a lack of touch. The untouched wither; the touched thrive. It means everything to be touched, to feel a gentle caress. We live through the sensations felt in our skin as much as through the sights and sounds detected by our eyes and ears. To not want touch is an indication of pathology—some cognitive impairment or a history of the abuse of this essential human act. Our bodies long for connection; we long to be present with one another.

Our flesh craves an economy of life that reaches beyond simple exchange, buying, and selling. Touch is to be a gift.

Cultures are built through gifts, anthropologists tell us. To give a gift implies relationship and a desire for mutual good. Enemies do not exchange gifts. Our bodies were our first gifts, given to us by God and our parents, and given by us to others through our touch. I don't mean only the sexual gift of our bodies. There is also the broader gift of embracing each other, like arms joined in a dance. It is easy to imagine our ancestors' feet moving around some ancient fire in the joy of being embodied together. Prostitution is called "the oldest profession," and though I imagine this was not the case, such a mythic history shows that the foundational gift of touch can quickly be drawn into the perverse economy of fixed exchange. Many people are willing to buy—and worse, to take—what is not given.

A lonely body that is not touched is quick to spread its loneliness to the soul. It will sacrifice a better knowledge to meet the satisfaction of the skin. And so loneliness is a problem not only of the body but also a problem of the soul. Even when everything else is good and right in heart and mind, the body can lead the whole person into a desperate loneliness if its longings are unsatisfied.

The church should be a place where we remember our bodies and learn the communion of touch. It is in the church that we eat and taste the earthbound flesh of Christ: the body and the blood of communion. It is in the church that we anoint the sick with the touch of oil on the forehead in a cross-shaped gesture. It is in the church that we baptize the body in water, immersing the new believers by lowering them into the baptismal pool or by taking handfuls of water from a font and pouring it over their heads. "Greet one another with a holy kiss"

(Romans 16:16), says Paul. This exhortation is cultural, of course, but it also communicates a basic need for the church to be a place of healing touch and of bodily embrace.

There is the holy unction of oils drawn in a cross on the forehead; the body of Christ pressed down, in the Eucharist, into the hand or placed on the tongue. Touch in all these acts is sacramental. There is also the washing of feet, an experience both tender and uncomfortable. I mourn for those who cannot let their bodies come forward to be served and to serve the body, as Christ served the bodies of his followers.

To some these acts seem dangerous, even scandalous. There are some who see foot washing and communion—the eating of Christ's body and blood—as being somehow erotic, and though these acts are not sexual in the common sense of the word, they are certainly filled with a kind of love that desires the other. When we eat the Eucharist, the church gathered together around this meal, we desire to be with Jesus in a deep and fundamental way. And Jesus, the Gospels seem clear, desires to be with us in body. He told his disciples that the place where they could find him was in the breaking of bread and in fellowship, people coming together in the flesh, around a table.

Jesus also taught that when we come alongside the bodies of those in need—those in prison, those who are sick—we are with him. We are with him when we clothe the bodies of those who need clothing, when we feed the bodies of those who are hungry. It is in touching that flesh, these bodies, that we touch God. This is the truth in the loneliness we feel: we long to touch and to be touched by God. But we don't always recognize the name and object of our longing, so we seek only the flesh that will bring an end to it.

For me that longing found its answer in Liz.

Under the bright, cool blue sky of an Arkansas fall, Liz and I joined other Natural State Expo volunteers in setting up in the big convention space. When it came time for lunch, we carried takeout to the park for a picnic. Liz told me that she had ended things with the other guy—no hard feelings, it hadn't been serious.

I grabbed her hand, and we walked like that—the lines and creases of our palms joined—everything suddenly bright and clear. Deep in my self I felt hope and possibility, my life facing a new sunrise. We were together at last, and the loneliness I'd long felt was swallowed up by the excitement of new touch, conversation, and ready love.

In the months that followed, I let go of the anxieties that had once held me back. In all my sexual experiences up to that point, I'd felt conflict between the now and the later. In the now—my body against another's, explosions of synapses and hormones, the hundred-million-year force of evolutionary drive. I wanted nothing more than *that* body, all of that body.

But there was also the later—sex was a mistake, an irresponsible abuse of the sacred connection that I felt should be bound by a serious vow of love. Before Liz I had played around the borders of sex, and when I gave in was always conflicted. Later I would say, "I won't do it again," but of course I did.

Thomas Merton wrote in his classic work *New Seeds of Contemplation:* "Chastity is not possible without ascetic self-sacrifice in many other areas. It demands a certain amount of fasting, it requires a very temperate and well-ordered life."[21] There is much truth in that idea, and my life at that time was far from ascetic and in no way well ordered. The only chance people have to overcome lust of any kind—be it for money or violence or sex—is to train our bodies to wait.

Remember all those youth group kids who were taught not to play with bear traps or wildfires? A better path toward sexual responsibility would be to train the whole person to be able to answer the call of love, not with the immediate drives of the body, but rather with the endurance of the body: the ability to keep moving toward some distant goal even when everything else says stop and give in and give up. The apostle Paul, who knew this discipline well, said it this way: "We also boast in our sufferings, knowing that suffering produces endurance, and endurance produces character, and character produces hope" (Romans 5:3–4).

At the time I met Liz, both my body and my soul were out of shape. I didn't have the character required to go long and wait. And so, just as I decided to forget about the scales and health and keep eating whatever I wanted, I decided I would let go and no longer live in feelings of conflict between my immediate wants and some greater good. Liz was a lapsed Catholic who'd had some meaningful experiences of faith in college but had since set those experiences aside. When we met, she said she wanted to explore her spirituality more, but nothing ever came of it for either of us. We both lacked the patterns of living that would have allowed any real spiritual transformation to take root.

In college one summer I read St. Augustine's *Confessions*. In the story of Augustine's path to faith, I recognized an echo of my own. Augustine confessed that, though his mind sought what was noble, his body was consumed with lust. His mind and spirit became convinced of the truth of Christianity, but he was not able to bring his body along at first. He prayed, "Lord, make me chaste but not just yet!"[22]

Even after Augustine made the move to bring his body into the faith, he continued to struggle with how to make sense of his flesh. Many people blame Augustine for some of the troubled understandings of the body that exist within the Christian faith. Even after Augustine was able to become chaste, he was unable to make full sense of the desiring, sexual aspects of his body. I do not fault him for this. I understand the struggle. In my relationship with Liz, though I had grown up in the faith, I felt that I had come to a decision point, saying, "Yes, but not yet!" I knew that I was called to sexual responsibility within the limits and bounds of a sacramental marriage, but God's will would have to wait until I was happy.

———

God interrupts, crashes in, reasserts the divine into our life. This happens not simply so that God can get our attention; it is reality coming to bear, as reality will eventually do. For Liz and me, reality arrived while she was in Asia, training staff for Heifer International. Her period was late, and she felt some nausea.

She searched Hong Kong for a pregnancy test, and those strange blue crosses appeared on the test strip. At the time, I was on a weekend trip volunteering for a sustainability camp. It was a warm March day, spring just emerging from the winter, when I got the call. I walked along the edge of the mountain on which the camp sat, raptors twisting on the warm air rising from the valley. Liz sounded confident, sure and calm. She was pregnant. She loved me. She wanted to have this baby with me. My carefully knit plans were now unraveled threads that spilled out in all directions. I walked with my friend Nathanael to the open-air chapel of the camp that looked out over the valley below.

"Liz is pregnant," I told him shakily. I felt in my whole self a mix of shame and excitement, wonder and dread.

Nathanael, the son of an Episcopal priest, helped guide my shock into happiness, in his nonchalant way: "You're going to have a little baby," he said, "That's awesome." And I realized that it *was* awesome—a new life on its way—whatever else might come.

Before I left for home that weekend, I asked the camp director to pencil in a date for a wedding. Liz and I would be married in this beautiful place, just a mile from where my farm was winding down. "We live the given life, and not the planned," Wendell Berry wrote in one of his Sabbath Poems.[23] My plans had ended and now I had to live into this gift, in all of its uncertainty.

Liz's plane landed two weeks later. I brought flowers to the airport. Her pregnant body was jet lagged and exhausted after the sleepless distance. We ate dinner at a bar and grill where I knew the chef, and then we took a sunset walk in a park unfamiliar to either of us. From an overlook on a hill we watched the sunlight dim against the city, the pink haze reflected off of green sprouting leaves, the city bathed in the last bit of western light before the power flickered on and all went fluorescent.

I pulled out a ring, simple and classic, and offered it to her as we looked out at the fading horizon. My yes became her yes. We would get married. We loved each other, and in that love we would raise the small life growing inside of her. We went back to her house and made love. On any other night we both would have smoked or had a drink, but this time while I did, Liz didn't. She was moving into the responsibility of motherhood, her "Yes" turned toward the life inside her as much as it was turned toward me.

Our vacation from responsibility and from faith was over. We wanted to be married by a priest, and so we had to find one. Our lives and bodies had come together for pleasure more than for anything else; we enjoyed each other and wanted each other. But now another life had joined us—part of my body and part of her body now living inside her—and we wanted somehow to make holy the baby's growing life.

It was almost Easter. Everywhere the world was blossoming.

Ironman 70.3 Triathlon

Before daybreak
Branson, Missouri

The floodlights glare through the fog. Everywhere there is the sound of pressure valves popping as bike tires are pumped past 120 psi. Athletes move around putting helmets on handlebars, checking bike computers one more time, laying bike shoes out carefully on brightly colored towels. Chains are lubed again after yesterday's rain, the threat of its return still hanging in the air. People are strangely quiet, despite the pump-you-up mix of rock and rap blaring from the loudspeakers. The athletes have a monk-like concentration.

It is 6 a.m. In an hour the horn will blare, and the first wave of athletes will rush into the cold September waters of Table Rock Lake to swim the 1.2 miles to start their 70.3-mile, Half Ironman day. I've never raced this distance. I've barely gone the distance of each of its segments: the 1.2-mile swim, the 56-mile bike ride, the 13.1-mile run. I picked Ironman Branson 70.3 because it was the closest 70.3 race to where I live. I didn't realize when I pushed "Register" that this is considered the most challenging bike course in the whole 70.3 series because of the hilly ups and downs of the Ozark Mountains. I hadn't yet read the words of the multiple-Ironman finisher, who posted on the triathlon forum Slowtwitch that he considered the Branson 70.3 as grueling as any full-distance Ironman race.

So here I am with my road bike and a body just now coming into some kind of fitness, about to spend the next six-plus hours pushing across water, up hills, and through a half marathon that is sure to leave my legs wrecked. I've been training, of course. I've been lifting weights, running sprint intervals, going out on regular group rides—desperately hanging on with a group of local guys far faster than me, their Zone 2, easy heart rates equaling my Zone 5, hard-as-I-can-go racing rate. I am as prepared as possible, but anything can happen in a distance race like this one.

Just down the row of bikes I see Bill. Bill and I went to high school together and have reconnected on hard group rides. He is a very fast marathoner, a regular on the podium in local running races. He took up triathlon earlier this year, and it wasn't long before his light, muscular body was pushing his bike to competitive speeds. His triathlon bike, a hand-me-down from a former pro-cyclist, is equipped with a new pair of expensive Aero race wheels. His equipment setup is competitive enough to enable him to race along any cyclist on the roads. I am here to finish; Bill, though he still needs more triathlon experience, has an honest chance of placing in the top ten of our age group.

Bill and I exchange subdued "hellos" and "good lucks," both of us maintaining the quiet concentration of race morning. I take my bike setup down to the beach to meet my parents and wife, who have come to cheer me through the day. I need to put on my wetsuit before the race starts, but I delay suiting up as long as possible; once it is on and zipped up there is no going back. I hit the portable toilets first. The line is long, many nervous stomachs making for a troubled morning. I've prepared, rising at 3 a.m. to eat breakfast and then going back to sleep. The calories are available in my body, fully processed. My body is as ready as it will ever be for this day, whatever it may bring.

I put BodyGlide around my wrists and ankles to make it easier for me to pull the wetsuit off later. With the help of my wife, I pull on the skintight neoprene that makes me look like a failed superhero. I take two calcium-based pills that are supposed to help with lactic acid buildup in my legs. I need all the help I can get, placebo or otherwise.

We make our way down to the beach, and I jump in the water to warm up, driving my body toward a buoy, practicing my stroke. The sun is rising over the water, giving off the purple hue of a post-rain dawn. The water is cold. I feel alive and free from my constant worries and anxieties. In a few minutes the horn will sound, and there will be nothing to think about but getting to the end, passing this rider or that one, adjusting my pace, shifting my gears on the hills to make for an easier climb—a thousand present moments.

The pros and some of the older age groups already started. Now comes the call for the thirty- to thirty-four-year-old men. There are forty or so of us, most in wetsuits and all of us with matching colored swim caps with our race numbers printed on the side. I kiss my wife, hug my parents, then walk to the start and dig my feet in the sand. Everyone talks about their pace. "How fast are you going to go?"

"Two minutes per hundred," one racer says. "One minute thirty," says another. We try as best we can to arrange ourselves according to pace; there's no sense in getting swum over or having to swim over a lot of other bodies. Most athletes overestimate their pace. I take that into consideration and get in the middle of the pack with those who say they are going to swim a little slower than I think I can. Bill is up ahead with some of the faster swimmers, and I know he shouldn't be. The one skill

I have in triathlon that's worth something is swimming. I'm not a racer, but I am steady. In local races I've recently started getting out of the water toward the front of the pack.

A moment later I see Bill walk past me. I wave, but his head is down. *He's going to a slower pace position,* I think. But then there's no time to think. The horn sounds, and we run into the water. I keep wide of the buoys at first, swimming past and through and over slower swimmers. I try to find open water and then I do, keeping a steady pace, not pushing it. I feel like I could go faster, but I hold back. This is a long day and now is no time to exhaust myself. We've started; the countdown of water and road to 70.3 miles has begun.

By the end of the day—my swim and bike ride over; my run halfway done—I'm sipping pickle juice almost constantly to ease the cramping in my legs. The thunderstorm that has been threatening since the morning, and has mercifully held off until after the hilly, fifty-six-mile bike segment, finally arrives. Big drops of rain fall like soft marbles, illuminated by all-too-close bursts of lightning. We are running next to a river. In normal life running by a river in a lightning storm would defy all wisdom. But I've come this far; there's no quitting now. *Six miles to go.* Lightning strikes don't happen often. It is rare that race organizers cancel due to weather, especially in a long race like a Half Ironman. People have trained for months, some have traveled across the country, and at this point in the day we've raced over half the distance. No one wants to stop, even in the face of lightning or hail or rain.

The rain has mostly subsided by the last mile. My legs are cramping bad, but I keep them moving—relentless forward progress, perpetual forward motion. I focus on every step, remembering consciously with every step how to run. *Lift, fall, catch. Lift, fall, catch.* I can hear the crowd at the finish line. I hear the announcer calling out the names of the other racers as they come into the finishing chute.

Then I see the finish line just up ahead, and I give everything left in my body, every last push of effort that I can pull from somewhere deep inside. I enter the chute and cross the mat that beeps as it registers the record of my race time. A crew waits at the end to help me stop; they'll catch me if I fall, which many athletes do when the relentless forward progress finally ends. They give me a silver thermal blanket. I reach into the big bin by the finish line and pull out a chocolate milk, a proven and favorite recovery drink for many athletes.

My parents and wife are there, all smiles and congratulations. I sit down on a bench. My body is weak and I feel emotional—a fog of joy and pain, overwhelmed at having finished.

"We are so proud of you," my father says. He's a little teary.

I spot Hilary, another athlete from my local triathlon club.

"Did you see Bill?" she asks me.

"No. I kept thinking I'd see him way out ahead on the bike, but never did."

Later, as we eat a post-race meal of pizza, I learn that Bill never started the race. He had all of the ability. He was strong and fast, but whether out of pride or fear or both, he didn't start that swim.

On the drive home my mom calls. She tells me again how proud she and my father are of me. And then she says, "Even if you hadn't finished, what I'm so proud of is that you started. You risked failure and you started."

Sometimes the start—the vulnerability risked in facing the possibility of not making it to the finish line—is the most important thing. Starting is how our bodies move into their futures. We can't learn to walk as infants without falls; scrapes and bruises are the evidence of our education. This is true of all the walks we take in life; to move, we have to take our chances with stumbling.

This Is My Broken Body

Liz and I lay on her bed in the midafternoon, the bright spring sun filtering through the closed curtains. We had plans to go out later to celebrate my twenty-eighth birthday. For now we were simply together, talking after love, dreaming of what the life inside her would be like and what our life together would become. The future seemed good and full.

Liz went to the bathroom, and when she came back, she said, "I'm spotting." We'd been reading about the risks and various stages of this new pregnancy. We knew that this could be nothing but that it could also be something. We waited and the spotting continued. Liz could feel in her body that something wasn't right.

Liz called her mother, a sweet woman who was into crystals and Indigo Children and meditating in geodesic domes. She told Liz to pray, to talk to her child inside and tell her that Liz wanted her—that she wanted the baby to live and stay and grow. And this is what Liz told our child, the size of a walnut, that despite the rush and doubts, Liz wanted her. With that prayer we went to a hospital early that night, the same hospital in which I had been born twenty-eight years earlier. We'd heard from the midwife we saw for Liz's prenatal visits that the hospital had a good neonatal ward.

But this wasn't a planned neonatal visit. In the bright, crowded emergency room we waited among poor families who had no other choice than the guaranteed care of an "emergency" to get their health care needs met. After four hours we were walked beyond the door to a sterile room. "A doctor will be in to see you," we were told. We kept waiting in our worry.

I looked at the brochures about blood pressure and the drug company literature displayed on the wall. Liz and I were tired, and we were both lost in our own imaginations, playing out the possible scenarios before us. I hated all of the sterile surfaces, the potential procedures, the mechanical efficiency of it all. I wanted someone to come and be present with us. I would have preferred an herb-and-incantation-offering witch doctor who was *with us* to the lonely wait for one more person with a clipboard.

A friendly nurse came and put cold, clear gel on Liz's now-showing pregnant belly. The speaker crackled as the nurse moved the monitor over Liz's skin, all of us straining to hear the fast thud of a heartbeat. Nothing. An aide put us on an elevator and took us to another floor where I was sent to a waiting room and Liz was ushered down the hall for an ultrasound. I sat among magazines filled with stories of the latest celebrity affairs; the TV was turned to E!. This is how we wait for life or death—for healing or the sad prognosis of disease—with *People* and paparazzi.

When Liz returned, she confirmed what she and I had been realizing. The life inside of her—*our* life inside of her—was over. Next came the agonizing process for her of delivering this interrupted life. Later, we held each other as we walked out into the early dawn. We were too tired to really understand and accept all that had happened. We drove to breakfast beneath the purple and pink of early dawn clouds.

Inside a faux log cabin, among country kitsch, we ate buttermilk pan-cakes and bacon together; a strange way to mark an end, but a human one. Together and tired, we sought comfort in the salt, fat, and syrup.

"We're in love. It's not about the baby. We would be getting married anyway." We had repeated those words many times to ourselves and to concerned friends and family who asked. Now, with no baby to bind us to our word, we had to decide how much we were going to live up to it. The ring was on Liz's finger, the wedding chapel reserved. We'd been going to premarital counseling. The momentum was with us.

But Liz was beginning to have doubts, to feel like she wanted to slow down the process. I am a get-it-done person, a move-it-forward person who will stick with a commitment through all kinds of misery. Now that we were heading toward marriage, I wasn't about to give up. I convinced her with my best sales pitch that everything would be okay. I lacked the humility to quit and the wisdom to see that the trauma of miscarriage in April would give weight to the option of postponing a wedding scheduled for May. Exhausted, Liz allowed herself to be pulled along by my energy. I ordered the cake and arranged the wedding web-site. She only had to show up and say "I do." She was depressed and confused; I was energetic and certain. We were a bipolar pair, each of us dealing with the tragedy of our loss in different ways.

Then there was my body, the body that would soon be bound to her by obligation if not by choice. She had seen the old pictures. She knew that I hadn't always been so fat. "Didn't your ex-girlfriend say something about you gaining weight?" Liz asked one day when we were in bed. I cried and told her that I'd been trying, but that this had been a lifelong struggle. I asked her to simply love me as I was, and she didn't say anything more.

But then there was Chicago in spring, the air caught between cold, gray winter and the warm blossoms of May. Liz and I both considered Chicago our big city. We'd both been students there; we both knew the neighborhoods of the North Shore, how to get around on the CTA, and the best places to eat Thai. Chicago was where we had gone for New Year's Eve; we'd celebrated at a favorite dive bar, the Red Line Tap, and had drunken snowball fights the whole walk back to Alex's north Chicago apartment. In early May we went back to Chicago to meet up with friends and pick up Liz's wedding dress.

In the bars we visited I felt again the inadequacy of my body and clothes, weighing myself against the cool of those who knew better how to make themselves into objects of desire and want and interest. But now, unlike in those years before, there was no smoking in bars. There was no escape into a cigarette that could fill the awkward emptiness and silence.

One night, Liz and I sat at a table talking with some of my friends. We'd all been playing pool and, as usual, my friend Jamie was winning most games. I wore a large plaid shirt. Talk turned to the topic of all that had changed—like our hairlines, jobs, and relationships—in the few years since we'd all lived in the same city.

"Few of us have changed as much as Ragan," one friend said, as if he'd been thinking about it for a while. We all knew what he meant: the seventy plus pounds I'd gained. There was an awkward pause before someone mercifully transitioned the conversation to something else.

My weight had become the unavoidable fact of "me" no matter what room I was in. I was no longer the blue-eyed guy with the ready smile; no longer the guy in the red plaid shirt, the guy with the beard. I was noticeably and undeniably the "big guy," and not in a ripped linebacker way; I was "big" in the euphemism-for-fat-guy kind of way.

Suddenly, the fact that I was the "big guy" started to sink in with Liz, and she started to look past my cool as a writer and farmer and local food activist and see me as the "big guy" more than anything else. Most of her friends had never met me, and she began to see me with their eyes, new and strange outside the context of our story. She and I no longer had the kind of conversations that had made us yearn for more, our phone calls lasting late into the night. It was hard to remember the moment when our relationship began, when we'd held hands on a fall day beneath a sky so blue it felt like a shade of infinity. Instead I was becoming "the fat guy"—an object she would be bound to like a heavy anchor against the flow of an otherwise happy life.

We talk a great deal these days about objectifying bodies, and by that we usually mean the bodies our culture holds up as objects of desire: magazine models, airbrushed and blemish-free. But we objectify bodies and people in more ways than that. We reduce people to objects when we see them as selves without a story. It is our stories that make us who we are; it is through story that we experience others as subjects and not objects.

When we see people without recognizing that they have a story, we become pornographers. Pornography almost by definition lacks a story. As soon as a film starts to develop characters, giving them backgrounds and contexts, it begins to move away from the pornographic. Pornographic films require just enough story to make the desire portrayed seem real—and no more. Once a film starts to become about something else, to become the story of a *person* with an infinite soul behind the makeup, it becomes difficult to see that person as only a thing provided to serve someone's needs. We must hold on to stories; these are what protect our ability to recognize the infinite in others. Without stories we are doomed to fall into the solipsism that makes us the master and center of our tiny universe.

There has been a move in recent years to rehabilitate the Gnostics —to reclaim the idea that there are more kinds of Christianity than the kind that came down through the institutional church. This is a narrative that plays well and sells well, especially since the riddle-laden and obscure language of the Gnostics can be reinterpreted as a New Age narrative. The narrative is one of personal empowerment and salvation that has little to do with the hard work that comes with embodying a faith.

I once took a graduate-school class that addressed one of the most popular of the Gnostic texts: the Gospel of Thomas. The Gospel of Thomas is a collection of sayings that are attributed to Jesus. Some of these sayings are versions of familiar texts found in the New Testament; others directly contradict the New Testament witness. What is really different about the Gospel of Thomas, however, is not its content but its form.

There is no story to the Gospel of Thomas. It presents a series of teachings reportedly delivered by Jesus, but these teachings are detached from the life and story of the Jesus who walked the dusty roads of Galilee, fasted in the sweaty heat of the desert, and was baptized in the silty waters of the Jordan. In the Gospel of Thomas, there is nothing about God washing dirt-caked feet that smell of road and leather. There is nothing about tears of blood or about bread that is broken. There is nothing about crucifixion or a resurrected Christ who asks for food and drink. In the Gnostic gospels there are only riddles and esoteric teachings that are meant to free the spirit from the lowly reality of the physical world. I want a God who bleeds real blood that turns red in oxygen. I want gospels that help me feel flesh, taste blood, and worship a God who healed eyes and hemorrhages, a God whose body was stabbed by nails and spears and then resurrected to walk side by side with his disciples.

A story requires incarnation. It requires time and flesh and birth

—and death hanging somewhere in the background. The Gnostics considered all of these things the basest parts of life, the lowest emanations of a pure ideal. The wisdom they favored was disembodied by design; putting aside the body was their aim and goal. God's purpose then was not to make the world holy but to rescue his people from the world. That is not the Christian story; like us, God has a body.

Pornography and Gnosticism follow similar roads. Both are about bodies without story or soul. We need to hold on to our stories, to listen to them, and to read them. Everybody has a story, from the first gasp of air. Even a drop of blood or shaft of hair can tell a geneticist the story of a person's history. Our narratives are deep and layered and varied. They echo our lives as creatures formed by a God who called these bodies "good." We must listen to these stories soon and listen fast. Once we lose the story, we lose the flesh of the God-come-here.

As I became known more and more as the "fat guy," my story was stripped away. As Liz lost her grip on that story, she began to see me as an object that did not satisfy her desire. This didn't happen in one instant; it was a progressive deletion. But moment by moment the text of my life began to fade, leaving only a still image of a guy who had seventy pounds to lose.

As we became objects to each other, Liz and I also behaved like objects that were being pushed forward by the forces of inertia we'd long ago set in motion with our rings and "Yeses." We were married on a beautiful spring day. The Arkansas heat bore down on me, hot in my black suit. Friends and family came, and our reception featured local food and a swirling dance where fiddles, dulcimers, and guitars kept time together. Liz cried at the exchange of vows, but only she knew that they were tears of fear and confusion and not joy.

I loved her and I think that she loved me, even as we came to see each other more and more as objects. We had both loved the long conversations of our early relationship. She longed deeply for a better world, and she had a joyful longing for adventure that was infectious. She loved to learn about people, especially the elderly, and spent long hours asking my willing grandparents for story after story about their lives. We shared a vision for a more sustainable life. We loved food, and we loved to cook elaborate meals together. And so we both said our "I do's" based on those memories and the history of all the things we'd loved together and the things we'd loved about one another, hoping for their return.

But in the same way she started to lose my story, I began to lose hers. In our disconnection, she had become a person without depth to me, an object to move along in my own story. I had longed to marry someone to escape from the sorrow of loneliness, and she was someone I had imagined stepping into my vision for a happy life. On our wedding night, despite not seeing each other as the people we really were, we danced and laughed with friends and celebrated as we were supposed to celebrate. Everyone had a good time.

After our families had returned home and the celebrations had faded, we woke up in our new apartment together. Sunlight streamed through the big window over our bed; framed pictures stood against the wall, waiting to be hung; boxes of wedding gifts lay in neat piles ready to be put away. As we ate breakfast together at the table, Liz watched me.

"Why do you lean over your plate like that?"

I'd never before noticed how I ate. No one had ever pointed it out as unusual to me, but she began to fixate on it. Another day, we sat together on our big front porch with its light-blue ceiling designed to keep the mosquitoes away. Liz looked at my legs, my thighs pushed out against the seat of the chair.

"Don't sit that way. It makes your legs look fat." I shifted in my seat, embarrassed by my butt and thighs and the seemingly feminine pattern in which my fat seemed to accumulate there.

Small comments like these began to accumulate. By the time we were in Belize for our honeymoon a week later, touring Mayan ruins and looking for toucans in the rainforests, Liz had begun to wonder aloud if our marriage could be annulled. We didn't make love even once that week, though we tried to make the best of foreign travel to a beautiful part of the world. Liz later said that it had been a fun vacation but only that. Everywhere I sat—from the crowded bus to the eco-resort where we started our tour of the country to the small boat we took to one of the islands off the coast—my weight and body inserted themselves as an issue.

"How about you sit here, big guy?" the bus driver said, trying to squeeze us all in.

"You get on this side," the boat captain pointed.

I wore T-shirts into the water, aware of how my body looked in contrast to the bodies of the beach-built college students all around us.

Over the following months Liz and I tried, off and on, to make it work. We escaped together into food; cooking was the only place where we fell into some pattern of common cooperation. We sat on the couch watching *Mad Men* together. We both found meaning in our work, and we invited our friends into our home so that we wouldn't have to be alone together.

But Liz sought more and more time away from me, going out often with friends. Occasionally we still made love, but this was mostly an exercise in frustration. We tried couple's therapy, but the therapist was no magician. I remained for her an object outside of her story, and she continued to be for me an object that I tried to draw into my own. With time I realized that the telling of my story wasn't up to me; that I was not the author of my life. My attempts to create a narrative that would end in my happiness had failed, and it was time for me not to tell, but to get told.

———

In my desperate, broken body, I began to hunger again for the healing food of Christ's broken body. I needed the gospel, some good news in my life that would draw me into a meaningful story. I started attending church at a little Episcopal parish hidden off a highway in suburban Little Rock. The priest there was the one who had married Liz and me; his sermons were good and the people kind. Liz attended a couple of times with me, but for the most part I went alone.

I said the prayers again, knelt for confession, passed Christ's peace to those around me. I sang along with the organ, stretching my vocal chords. I crossed my forehead, my lips, and my heart in little motions before the gospel was read. I prayed that God would fill my heart, mouth, and mind with the good news of God's grace. I knelt, holding my hands open to receive the bread whose ingredients had been grown in a soil formed from the decay of many deaths. I ate the broken body of Christ and drank his blood in that ancient ritual designed to join my body with his body.

In all of this I began to let God be the author of my story. The yarn I'd been trying to spin ceased to be my own. Instead I began—in fits and starts, with improvisations and tangents—to become a part of a bigger story. It was a story of salvation and of resurrection. It was a story of bodies that are good and mortal and everlasting, bodies that matter. It was a story that began on Sunday and lingered throughout the week.

In the weekly Eucharist I sought to connect my body to the flesh that was the Word, the story of us all. This Word was the Logos—Christ in whom we live and move and have our being. The early Christians understood him to be the ordering and creative principle of all things, the grammar of everything living and dead. From the moment Christ became flesh, the universe ceased to be a kind of abstraction that could make sense outside the context of a story. In him, all becomes story.

My body, broken and unraveling, returned to that flesh-word and became a part of the story of reconciliation once again. By going to church week in and week out, by reading the Scriptures and offering prayers, I let my story fade into this story of good news for all people. The failed narratives and brokenness of my body began to be retold with a different story than the one-dimensional word of rejection. I was now called to love, no matter what. This was not heroic love but the love of a follower, mimicking the love I saw played out in Christ. In that love I found what had been the source of my longing.

8 Weeks to Ironman

8:00 a.m.
East of Little Rock, Arkansas

David is in his sixties. He's lean and fit, but if you saw him on the street in civilian clothes you'd let stereotypes get in the way. His hair is gray, and he's mostly bald on top. He drives a minivan that is old and average, except for the Ironman symbol on the back. Open up the back of that van, and you'll see a mobile triathlon training center: a place to lay his bike and little cabinets with drawers and cubbies where he can store training gear.

Strip David down to his spandex bike clothes, and you'll see a body that's been racing and training for triathlons for almost as long as I've been alive. He's been in this sport since the eighties, close to the time when the first Ironman launched as a bet among fitness enthusiasts in Hawaii. Back then it was a contest designed to see who was fittest: runners, cyclists, or swimmers. To decide, the organizers combined the distances of Kona's three separate endurance events into one big endurance challenge: a 2.4-mile swim, a 112-mile bike, and the Kona marathon. The prize for the winner was nothing more than a six-pack of beer and the title "Ironman."

We gather at the back of David's van in the early fall dawn. The weather is still summer-like in Arkansas, where the heat can still reach above ninety in September. There are Heather, Pat, me, and a handful of others. Most of us are training for Ironman Florida, but I'm the only first-timer. Heather and David both have multiple finishes to their names, and Pat raced his first the year before this one. David is the organizer of this ride; he'll lead us through eighty miles of his training territory, the roads that stretch just east of Little Rock.

The ride starts out easy enough. We make our way through neighborhoods, riding carefully over the railroad tracks that are the bane of all cyclists. Then we hit the long, flat open roads that run through the Arkansas Delta. There are fields of soybeans and cotton; the remains of old cotton gins dot the landscape against the open sky. We pass fragments of the forests that are the native heritage here, cypress trees that are as old as Christianity growing along the bends of rivers and swamps that never lent themselves to clearing for crops.

After our muscles are warm we start going fast, pushing twenty-five miles an hour. David easily leads the way, a big smile on his face, snapping pictures of us as we ride. There are some athletes who train as a kind of masochistic act, always complaining about the hard days. One wonders why they do endurance events at all. Admittedly, there are hard days in any good training, but at its heart good training should also encompass the joy—like the joy of a fast ride in the wide open of the countryside. David embodies this joy of racing and riding. His life is not centered on the hard dream of winning (though he sometimes does win). David exudes the joy that comes with *going and going and going,* a pleasure only endurance sports can offer.

At first I can keep up the pace with no problem. I have speed and strength in my legs. But as the ride wears on past fifty miles, once we've been going for over two hours, I find myself struggling more and more to keep up. Fitness is a matter of modes—strength and agility, endurance and speed; someone who is fast or strong doesn't necessarily have endurance. There are also the matters of pacing and experience; these mean everything in longer races, like Ironman. Whereas most sports are games designed for twenty-somethings, the Ironman triathlon is a sport that rewards experience. Many of the top pros peak in their late thirties; the course record at the Ironman World Championships in Kona, Hawaii, was set not by some twenty-year-old, but by thirty-eight-year-old Craig "Crowie" Alexander.

Come November, I am going to have to ride more than eighty miles and *then* run a marathon. It is clear to me now that I need to train endurance into my body. Speed and strength will only help so much. I need the ability to keep going and going without stopping.

I hang on to the group, keeping up with them until we reach the parking lot where we gathered. From there I bike the three miles back to my house, my quads aching with the burn of muscle, the space-age polyesters of my cycling jersey soaked with sweat. I have work to do, but there is time.

I've endured before.

This Is My Body in the Desert

Even as our marriage spiraled downward, Liz and I experienced some moments of tenderness. Yet our lives were spent mostly apart. We were roommates more than we were a couple. I moved into the guest room, and that act of separation began the process of our slow walk away from each other. Liz went to marriage therapy with me, mostly out of obligation. There were tears and talk. But in the end, the therapist told Liz that she had made up her mind before she ever walked into that office. She suggested that we begin a trial separation to see if our feelings would change.

So Liz moved out, and I stayed in our lonely duplex, bare walls where the pictures had once hung. Our therapist instructed us to avoid all contact with each other until six months was up. We would then meet again in therapy to see how time had affected our feelings. Perhaps absence would bring a clarity that presence had not.

Shortly before Liz left, I walked with her to work; it had become harder and harder for us to find time to talk together. In the twenty minutes of that walk, we talked about our marriage. She explained why she wanted out; I explained why I wanted her to stay.

"I just can't be attracted to your body," she said.

"I'm working on getting my body in shape," I said. "You need to work on getting your *soul* in shape." It was an angry comeback, but there was truth in it, for me as much as for her. I was coming to understand that I needed both my body and my soul to be in shape together. This was not so I could develop an *O Magazine*–type spirituality or achieve the six-pack abs pushed in *Men's Health*. I wanted a body and soul that were ready to meet the challenge of love. Liz and I trying to love each other in the midst of all we were struggling through was a bit like us having been dropped into a marathon without training. I needed to learn to run, but I was already in the middle of the race.

—————

In the early days of Christianity—after the catacombs and bloody martyrs of the coliseums, at a time when Christianity was widespread and slowly becoming the religion of the Roman empire—groups of men and women went out to the desert to pray and fast and fight the devil. They were called *ascetics,* a word that came from the Greek *askesis*—meaning "to train or to exercise," a term that applied to athletes. These desert monastics weren't training for the new body of a marathoner or wrestler but for a new humanity. For them this was only possible by seeking Christlikeness. Christlikeness meant renewing humanity by returning it to God's original intentions for it—before Adam and Eve met the serpent, before the Fall, and before life outside of Eden began.

The Egyptian bishop Athanasius—a fiery, red-headed theologian—learned from these desert monastics. From that learning he articulated a vision for exactly what had happened when God became human, when the Word took on flesh. Athanasius argued that Jesus had come to re-create a humanity that had slipped into de-creation, people's lives no longer rooted in their divine source. In this way, there was no distinction "between salvation and creation." To save humankind was to re-create it, to call it back into being from nonbeing.

"I'm half the man I used to be" goes the old Stone Temple Pilots song, and the ascetics believed exactly this: that sin eats away at what is truly human and leaves us as hollow half-persons. As they saw it, Christ came not to save us with a hand reached down to pull us up from the pit, but by creating a new mold, a new model of what a human being should be. It was for this that the ascetics were training. To be in shape, for Athanasius and the desert monastics, was to be like Jesus because Jesus *was* the new shape.

What those monks were doing in the desert was seeking humanity's return to lives fully directed toward God. Far from despising the world, they were working to renew it. They did this by becoming more like Christ, the new shape for humankind. They took on many disciplines, including prayer and fasting and all-night vigils. They lived in communities with others, which forced them to learn to get along. They practiced celibacy. None of these activities, which are activities of the body as much as they are of the spirit, were meant to be good in and of themselves. These spiritual disciplines were training tools, like sprints run on a track or weight training done before a marathon. But their goal wasn't to become fast or strong in body; it was to embody a new humanity.

As Athanasius recounts it in his *Life of St. Anthony,* the old Abba Anthony appeared in a nearby village after years spent disciplining his body and spirit in the desert. Upon seeing him, the people were struck by his remarkable health: "When they beheld him, they were amazed to see that his body had maintained its former condition, neither fat from lack of exercise, nor emaciated from fasting and combat with demons, but was just as they had known him prior to his withdrawal. The state of his soul was one of purity."[24]

His face, many remarked, was like that of a child: completely transparent and open, appearing honest and good, with nothing to hide. He had become an example of that new humanity that the ascetics desired, one that is perhaps the secret desire of us all. We sense decay in ourselves, but we wish to be renewed in our humanity. Sex and six-pack abs won't give us that. We have to train for something else. Something harder, but more rewarding.

⌣

As my marriage fell apart, I had to go to my own kind of desert—not to escape but to become new. I had to return to health in soul and body. My metabolism was rocketing me toward diabetes; my fat gain the result of sugar-fueled binging. My soul, too, reflected the disordered pieces of a self. I was no heroic monk, but I *was* in need of a new self. I needed re-creation and salvation not just for my spirit, broken as it was, but also for my sick and addicted body. I began to carve out for myself a disciplined life that was formed by exercises of prayer and study and food and fitness, all in equal measure.

My days were shaped first by the old red *Book of Common Prayer* I'd bought in college and had practiced with, off and on, ever since. In daily Morning Prayer I found a practice that required nothing more of me than showing up. I didn't need to muster the concentration needed in contemplative prayer or the heart-filled emotion of real intercession. I simply had to say the prayers, and there was much healing in that.

When I eventually began to exercise my body, it was only after I had found something similar to Morning Prayer—a training plan I just had to show up for and do. Go pray, go exercise, read your Bible, eat right. None of these practices work regularly if doing them is dependent on a decision made in the moment. People need a regular plan and pattern to just show up for and fall into. The ancients of Israel knew this. They had their own collection of daily prayers and praise; the book we call Psalms was their prayer book. My *Book of Common Prayer* and every good prayer book since is based on the psalms. The Desert Fathers and Mothers would have had all of the psalms memorized from frequent reading and practice.

In the 150 biblical psalms can be found every emotion experienced by humans—from exalted joy and love to complete existential alienation. When Jesus felt abandoned by God on the cross, it was to the words of the psalms that he turned: "My God, my God, why have you forsaken me?" (Psalm 22:1; Matthew 27:46; Mark 15:34). In the psalms can be found the hottest anger and unleashed rage. There are images of such frank violence that modern readers often skip the verses that contain them. Having never lived in a place so close to war that there is blood in the streets, contemporary readers often feel ill-prepared to reconcile these calls for violence with the God of love they have come to know. But this desire for violence, whether we like it or not, is also a deep human feeling and, like all our feelings, must be offered to God.

The psalms are also rich with hope and faith and love; they are full of the joy the human heart finds in God. If a subject or object has anything to do with being human it can be found in the psalms—and that includes our bodies. There are over a thousand references to the body in the book of Psalms. Out of the 150 psalms, 143 make reference to the body. This poetry is concrete, filled with images of eyes seeing, hearts aching, and tongues praising. Biblical scholar Susanne Gillmayr-Bucher writes, "The persons in the Psalms do not so much have a body, they rather are a body."[25] In praying those psalms I began to see my torn and broken flesh as something glorious in intention and being.

> My flesh and my heart may fail,
>> but God is the strength of my heart and my
>> portion forever. (Psalm 73:26)

Therefore my heart is glad, and my soul rejoices;
　　my body also rests secure. (Psalm 16:9)

For it was you who formed my inward parts;
　　you knit me together in my mother's womb.
　　(Psalm 139:13)

As I learned again to pray during this desert time, I began also to engage my body in another way. For years I had started (and quit) several exercise programs. I tried to ride my bike, and I sometimes ran, but I felt out of breath after a quarter mile—my lungs compromised by smoking, my body heavy on my feet. I had no consistent rhythm, no daily routine of exercise. As is the case with any human activity worth doing, routine is the foundation for getting good.

We live in a culture that values spontaneity, if only because such a value works in the favor of compulsions to buy, to eat, and to consume. But spontaneity doesn't work if the goal is growth. Life runs on rhythms; order is unavoidable. My rhythm to that point had been to drive, smoke, drink Red Bull, and stay up late watching *30 Rock*. Now in this desert time, as my body was finding its rhythm in prayer, I was also discovering new patterns of exercise.

It is difficult to find one's way with prayer if one does not have the help of a priest or pastor or spiritual director. Father Ed, the priest at the Episcopal church I had joined, served in all of these roles for me, offering me counseling and prayer and accountability in my search for a deeper soul life. In the same way, it is hard to break all of the old habits of an unhealthy physical life without the help of a trainer or coach. Lorrie was the one who gave me my start toward the healing of my body.

Lorrie was a longtime customer of mine at the farmers' market who was also a personal trainer. She had told me often, in the gentlest way, that she would be glad to work with me for barter. And so, with an occasional exchange for a few dozen fresh eggs and a few pounds of grass-fed beef and lamb, she became the trainer of my body. Lorrie started with an assessment, testing my flexibility and measuring my waist, finding the weaknesses and faultiness in my body. From this baseline she developed a regular exercise plan that was easy for me to follow—one that focused on mobility and strength, not aerobics.

Next, Lorrie addressed my diet, which she said was the real source of my weight gain. However, unlike many trainers trapped in the paradigm of calorie balance, Lorrie emphasized eating real food, particularly good meat, healthy fats, and fibrous vegetables. She steered me away from carbohydrates: grains, most beans, and anything that was processed or had added sugar. Fruit, she said, was a good natural dessert, but even it had to be eaten in moderation since it was full of sugar.

It was hard for me to accept this advice at first. For one thing, I prided myself on my abilities as a bread baker and a foodie. Cutting whole vast categories of food from my plate was a hard choice to make. Wouldn't it be easier to just eat a small amount of whatever food I wanted in moderation? I downloaded a fitness app and tracked my calories, following the app's recommendations regarding how many calories to reduce. I meticulously entered everything I ate into the program, yet I made virtually no weight-loss progress. I had not yet addressed the system of hormones that was contributing to making me fat. I needed to pay attention to not only the number of calories but also the kind of calories I was eating.

Still unwilling to accept such a restrictive diet, I continued to conduct my own diet research. The information I found confirmed the wisdom of Lorrie's approach and made sense to me as an ecologist and farmer. The emphasis on carbohydrates in the modern diet is a novelty; humans throughout most of history didn't eat grains, "whole grains" or not. Those who did certainly didn't eat the most refined sorts of carbohydrates commonly eaten today: white flour and white sugar and white potatoes. Writer Mark Sisson, on his blog *Mark's Daily Apple,* puts this truth in the simplest terms possible: "Carbohydrate drives insulin drives fat storage." As soon as I accepted that truth and acted accordingly, I began to lose weight, slowly at first and then significantly. Eventually I seemed to flip some kind of metabolic switch and my body shifted from "storing fat" mode to "burning fat" mode.

This truth about the effects of carbohydrates was like a revelation to me. And though my new way of eating required discipline, as does any form of eating, it eventually became more a lifestyle for me than a diet. I don't always stay true to this way of eating. But when the pounds start to come back, when my pants get a little tighter, then aligning myself more closely with this way of eating is a sure way for me to return to health. I've watched friends follow the same path. It has worked, and continues to work, for them and for me.

One of the most important insights to come out of this approach is this: the problem isn't me or you; it's our food. The problem is the sugar, which is toxic and addictive and shows up in our pita bread and our low fat bagels and in those tropical smoothies that make us feel like, in drinking them, we're doing something healthy. Fat isn't the enemy; sugar is, in whatever form it comes but especially in those products that promise that they are low fat, because they are then, instead, invariably high sugar as a result of manufacturers' efforts to replace the lost fat flavor with something else that tastes good.

Whichever of the disciplines I was focused on—prayer or exercise or eating—I found that there was one new lesson I had to learn again and again. I had to surrender. I had to surrender my mind and heart to the prayers. To bend my knees when the prayer book said to, to confess even when I didn't feel like it. It was the same with exercise. I had to submit to written plans that told me on Monday to jump rope a hundred times and do pull-downs and push-ups and bicycle crunches and on Tuesday to do Russian plyometric jumps and presses on a BOSU ball. With diet I had to surrender to the reality of my body. I had to accept that while others might have genetic gifts that allow them to eat a lot of starchy carbs without gaining weight, I can't because my body (like most bodies, really) can't handle more than around a hundred grams of carbohydrates a day without snowballing into obesity.

This lesson of surrender, the final secret to the real start of my health, came to me in a dream. I don't remember dreams very often, but I remember this one vividly. In the dream I was in the public library downtown, and I had checked out a book written by a man named E. Stanley Jones. His name was clearly visible on the spine. The dream was nothing more than that: I went to the library and I checked out a book.

Prior to the dream I had never read E. Stanley Jones, but I'm fairly sure I had heard him quoted a few days before it. Afterward, I researched Jones and found that he was a fascinating figure: a Christian missionary to India who had been friends with Gandhi, a confidant of Franklin Roosevelt who had urged the president to avoid war with Japan, and the author of a biography of Gandhi that Martin Luther King Jr. took with him everywhere he traveled and had in his briefcase the day he died.

Following my dream's leading, I went to the public library and typed Jones's name into the electronic catalogue. I wrote down all of the call numbers of his books and went searching among the stacks. One by one I looked for them, but I kept finding them missing from the shelves. Finally I came to the last call number, and there on the shelf was a thin book with a perma-bound cover: *Victory Through Surrender*. I checked it out and put everything else aside to read it. In its pages Jones had the message that I most needed to hear and live into:

> The surrender which seems downward, laying down your arms,
> is actually a surrender upwards. It is a surrender to creative love.

This is not acquiescence. It is cooperation with the power that raised Jesus from the dead—that power when surrendered to and cooperated with will raise us from a dead noncontributive life to a creative and fruitful one....

The one business of human living is to keep our wills coinciding with the will of God in self-surrender and constant obedience. When we do, the sum total of reality is behind us, we have cosmic backing for our way of life....

Everybody surrenders—surrenders to something, someone, or Someone.... We all surrender, from the moment two cells, the sperm and the ovum, surrender to each other to form a new life down to the moment where our bodies are surrendered to the grave.... We are free to choose, but not free to choose the results or consequences of our choices.[26]

I am not a superstitious Christian. I don't tend to go for stories of angels or dreams or God's words whispered on the wind. My faith is both more rational and more mysterious than that. God's word comes to me in the quiet revelations I experience when I read various writers and through the Scriptures I reflect upon. But in some mysterious way I had been led to this book, written by this writer, and those words were exactly what I needed just then.

Surrender was the secret I'd been missing, and Jones's words—delivered to me from across the decades—told me how to begin. Without surrender, I would never have begun to live healthily at last. Without surrender, I wouldn't have been ready, coming out of that desert time, to handle the journey of death and resurrection that was to come.

Ironman Big Day

Race rehearsal workout

I want a turkey sandwich. I don't know why, but after a long ride I always want a turkey sandwich: simple wheat bread, Bibb lettuce, thin-sliced meat, and mayo. These days I generally avoid bread, wheat, and grains of any kind, but when I've been exercising for six hours I allow myself a turkey sandwich. There are worse cheat meals.

Today started at 4:30 a.m. To start my day I fixed a banana smoothie with some chocolate protein powder mixed in. I tried to drink plenty of water but didn't focus on a specific number of ounces; I typically drink as much as my thirst demands, not according to some outside measure. Four-thirty is the time I will likely wake on Ironman race day, and today is a dress rehearsal. I won't work out at anywhere near the intensity that I will at Ironman; today is simply about getting a sense of the amount of time involved. I prepared my bike, my clothes, and my nutrition for my run. Then at 7:00 — race day start time — I swam for an hour in the pool before taking a ninety-minute break. By

9:30 I'd put on the same triathlon kit—shirt and shorts—that I'll wear on race day and had clipped my shoes into my tri-bike.

I rode my bike for five hours through the swampy flatlands east of Little Rock, the best approximation of the terrain I'll face in Florida that I can find around here. Along the way I ate Bonk Breaker bars and sipped from two bottles—one filled with a carbohydrate drink and the other with plain water. The carb drink is something I've been experimenting with, a new product that includes a "silky maize" starch. Ideally during a long race, the body will run on a mix of carbs and fat, but the theory among some physiologists like Timothy Noakes is that certain carbs can inhibit the body's ability to access stored fat. Racers may be able to counteract this effect by eating a relatively low-carbohydrate diet outside of race days. "Train low-carb, race high-carb" is common advice among athletes. Some people argue that racing low-carb works as well, but I haven't been able to train my body to do this yet. Sports gels and sports drinks always seem to give me the energy I need. This new drink is supposed to provide the carbs I need without the downside of an insulin spike.

As I pedaled I paid attention to my energy levels and my comfort, watching for any chafing of my clothes or aches and pains caused by my position on the bike. My shoulders began feeling tired toward the end of the ride. I made a mental note: *Talk to Scott at the bike shop about adjusting my aerobars a little farther forward.*

Now I'm home and my clothes are still soaked with sweat, but I don't change. I need to feel how they will wear over the whole day. During the Ironman I won't be able to kick back for an hour and a half and eat a sandwich like I'm about to do, but today isn't about putting out the same effort I will on race day. Today is about getting a feel for my equipment, my nutrition, and the time it will take to go from start to finish. It's a long time—eleven hours today, and that's short compared to my very best imagined Ironman race-day time. I'm not one of the fast guys.

Eating is a critical part of race training. Like everything else, eating has different seasons. Most of the time I tend to stick to the Paleo diet—the kind outlined in *The Paleo Diet for Athletes* that emphasizes pasture-raised meats, fish, and vegetables and includes no grains or refined sugar, except during limited windows of time when anything goes. I have friends who compete at high levels while eating a vegetarian diet, and this seems to work for them. Ultramarathoner Scott Jurek eats a vegan diet, though he has to eat a small farm's worth of vegetables to make it work. I can't say what is absolutely the best diet; each person needs to experiment to find what works best for his or her own body. What *is* key above all else is not eating junk, which is about 90 percent of readily available food. No refined sugar. No refined wheat flour. Nothing that took a scientist with a chemistry degree to manufacture in a food lab.

I shop often at an organic grocery store that stocks fresh, organic produce and generally sells no junk whatsoever. Sometimes I wear triathlon shirts when I go; after a person starts racing, pretty soon most of the T-shirts in his closet are race T-shirts. I often see other triathletes at the store, walking around in their own Ironman jackets and T-shirts, sunglasses perched on their heads, their legs shaved (both the men and the women). We nod in mutual recognition, one triathlete to another, and push around carts loaded with kale and kimchi and virgin coconut oil. We're all paying a higher price for this top-quality food than we would pay for products found at the average grocery store. Eating well costs more.

I'm not rich, at least not by relative American standards. I don't have a cable bill, I don't buy clothes very often, and I try to live pretty simply. But I do spend more on groceries than the average person. I do this in order to buy food that was grown with care, and that is free from the pesticides, antibiotics, and chemicals commonly found in the food that comes in cans, jars, and boxes. For me, it's all about priorities. As my friend Lorrie, the personal trainer, once said to me, "I have clients who complain about the cost of the food I ask them to buy and then drive away in a brand-new car. Aren't our bodies worth more than a new car?"

There are, of course, ways to get good food a little cheaper. Buying a whole chicken costs less per pound of meat than buying boneless breasts. Cooking with whole ingredients is often less expensive than buying premade and prepackaged products. I make a lot of food from scratch—from mayonnaise to spaghetti sauce. I also buy the cheaper options for meat—roasts, ground meat, canned wild salmon. All in all, I eat a quality diet without spending too much. I'll take the difference in costs elsewhere, like less money spent on doctors' bills and prescription drugs. I put a lot of work into taking care of this body, and it's important to me to give it the quality nutrition it needs.

In the afternoon of my race rehearsal day, I eat my turkey sandwich and then flip through *Triathlete* magazine while lying horizontal on the couch. I begin to drift off, the afternoon light streaming through the panoramic windows over the couch, but then my phone alarm rings with the sound of crickets—time to go.

I drive down to the River Trail, a long asphalt pedestrian trail that snakes along the Arkansas River. And then I run, the sun beating down on the open pavement, my body keeping pace on tired legs, fueled by the good food that has built these muscles. Two more hours and this training day will be done. Two more months and I won't be rehearsing anymore.

This Is My
Body Resurrected

Christianity is a religion of seasons. There is Advent, then Christmas (a season as well as a day), and then Epiphany; these are followed by Lent and Easter, Pentecost, and Ordinary Time. Each season has its own purpose; each has its disciplines and colors and sacred practices.

Advent and Lent are solemn and penitential, times for reflecting and going slow. Christmas and Easter are celebratory seasons, times in which we stand rather than kneel, we feast instead of fast. It is important to practice each season in the way it was intended; together these seasons round out our experiences of faith and life. If our spiritual lives are made up of all fasting and confession and penance, they will become too lean; if it's all feasts and bold approaches to God, our spiritual lives will become fat and cavalier. The act of moving through seasons forms us into complete people—harmonious and whole, capable of sustaining faith over the long run.

Like the church, the body too has seasons. To train well for going long, one must submit to seasons of training: seasons of easy and long training, seasons of hard and short, seasons of both together. First, there is a "base" period, during which the aerobic systems of the body are built and strengthened. This is the season of Zone 2, long and slow. Then comes a "build" season that finds the body climbing toward its best possible condition, preparing for the hardest workouts of the cycle. Next is the "peak" season, in which intensity reaches its apex and everything becomes about race-like training. Last comes the "taper," one or two weeks during which training slows so that the body can recover from the most intense work and be at its best for race day.

Ignore the seasons—the rhythms of body and soul—and one will likely be unprepared on the day when the results of training are needed. Without training I wouldn't have been ready for the day when Liz e-mailed and said she wanted to talk, five months into our planned six-month separation. Without seasons spent training my heart and soul for what was coming, I might have become lost in rage and jealousy and utter grief. It's not that I didn't feel all of those things; not that I didn't sense in my body a kind of sorrow that made food unappetizing and caused my shoulders to slump. But I was not lost in those feelings. I was able to push through them and open myself to the abiding, constant, overcoming love of God that was my only hope of salvation, my only possibility for re-creation.

My training for that final grief, and for the victory that followed that ultimate surrender, happened mostly during Lent. This was a time of fasting, of giving up the things that I had thought I needed for sustenance. In this way, I learned that the only true sustaining power of my life is the sparking surge beneath the creation: God who is in all and sustains all.

Lent is a time when Christians prepare for Easter season, remembering the forty days in the wilderness during which Jesus fasted; the forty days before the devil tempted him with power, fame, and the satisfaction of immediate desire. Many people read this story as one in which the devil tempts Jesus at his weakest: hungry and physically drained by his desert fasting. However, I think Dallas Willard is right when he writes in the *The Spirit of the Disciplines* that the wilderness "was actually *the place of strength and strengthening* for our Lord."[27] He has trained himself, during those forty days of fasting, to live in complete reliance on the power of God. At the time when the devil comes to him, Jesus has realized God's power as a full and present reality in his life. I did not have the same power as Jesus. But through the season of Lent I had become better prepared to show love in those times when I would find doing so to be the hardest.

Lent ends in Holy Week, a series of days during which Christians remember the journey Jesus took from the peasant countryside of his teaching ministry into Jerusalem, where he would directly challenge the religious and political authorities of the day. Holy Week starts with Palm Sunday, marking the triumphal entry when Jesus came into town with his band of social, religious, and economic outcasts. They were welcomed with hosannas and whispers among the crowds that the long-hoped-for Messiah had arrived.

On Palm Sunday I marched with the congregation of St. Michael's. We entered the nave with a haphazard triumphal entry of our own, waving the palms that we would later braid into small crosses. The palms would be kept until next year and then burned on Fat Tuesday, their ash becoming the char of Ash Wednesday that is applied in a cross-shaped smudge on the foreheads of worshipers. Palm Sunday is a day of celebration, but also of foreboding. We all know murder is coming by week's end.

The next day we gather during Holy Week is on Maundy Thursday. This is a commemoration of the Last Supper Christ had with his disciples, the night on which the master bent down and washed feet. It is called Maundy to echo the commandment Jesus gave to his disciples to love one another: Maundy meaning "mandate." This was the night that Jesus broke bread with his disciples, instituting the Eucharistic feast. Yet before any bread was broken or wine was poured, Jesus first wrapped a towel around his waist, kneeled down, and washed the feet of his disciples, each foot smelling of leather and sweat and street grime. In the Episcopal tradition we celebrate the Eucharist week in and week out. But it is only on Maundy Thursday that we wash feet. It is only on this day that we ritually serve each other in our humility.

Many people hold themselves back from this ritual; they are not comfortable with washing feet or with having their feet washed by others. Allowing oneself to receive this hospitality of foot washing requires vulnerability. This is as difficult for us now as it was then for Peter, who at first refused Jesus's gesture of servanthood. But on Maundy Thursday I feel a closeness that I feel at no other time in the church year. As we serve each other in this way, following Jesus's example of humility, we open ourselves up to community. When we wash one another's feet, the barriers of status and image are removed. This is what allows us to offer, and receive, the kind of open, ready-with-love hospitality that Jesus and the best of his disciples have modeled throughout the generations. In the days leading to my own Good Friday I experienced a season of Maundy Thursday—a time during which friends opened themselves up to me and shared their love.

Nathanael and his wife, Carrie, invited me to dinner on Valentine's Day. Katy and her new husband, Shelby, met me for Tex-Mex dinners and listened patiently to my troubles over chips and cheese dip. Shelby and Jonathan joined me for games of pool, beer specials, and conversations about everything from Cormac McCarthy's novels to NCAA basketball. Friends from church, even those who didn't know everything that was going on in my life, offered the quiet ministry of presence and welcomed me without questions into their worship.

These connections were what gave me the strength to meet Liz on the Friday of Holy Week. She e-mailed on Thursday and said that, though we still had a month before our separation was to end, she needed to talk right away. We met at the apartment we had once shared, then went on a long walk from there—the cool and sunny spring day filled with life against the death of winter, cumulus clouds towering against the dazzling blue sky.

As we walked, Liz said that the separation had been good for her but that her decision hadn't changed. She wanted out. She knew a lawyer who was helping her with the paperwork. We had little shared property; ending our marriage would be a fairly simple matter.

I had longed for some miraculous breakthrough, a divine reconciliation. Instead I was faced with the pain of loving even when my hopes weren't fulfilled. I told Liz that I was ready to do whatever I needed to do in order to reconcile, but that I wouldn't fight a divorce. We left it at that and wandered through the empty lots of a once-tornado-devastated neighborhood, where winter browns were starting to flash green with the promise of summer. As we walked we caught up on the minutiae of what had happened in our lives since the separation. I wouldn't see her much after that. There was some paperwork to complete and the division of a handful of co-owned belongings. It is strange how the promise for a lifetime can dissolve in the manner of one roommate leaving another, friends who will slowly forget each other over distance and time.

That evening, I drove the long highway out to St. Michael's, feeling the sadness of my marriage ending but also release from the burden of waiting. I had asked Father Ed to pray for my conversation with Liz. I met him in the hall before the Good Friday service.

"How was your talk?" he asked.

I answered simply that it was what I'd expected: she wanted a divorce.

"It is a kind of death," Father Ed acknowledged. "But you know what comes after death? Resurrection!"

The altar was bare, the lights low, as we ended that Good Friday in the dark knowledge that love came into the world and was murdered. But as we left the church, we also knew that in the holy silence of Saturday, God would work in a way far more powerful than any death. We knew that even as we mourned the crucified Christ, death could not keep him from loving us. We were called to remember that, in the same way, we must love in the face of the daily deaths that come our way—the loss of love and of loved ones, the betrayals that happen in a fallen world. We must learn, in the words of Wendell Berry, to "practice resurrection." We must live into the truth that God has come to raise us up and heal us from every kind of death.

Resurrection is a critical hope of Christians. People of many other faiths believe in reincarnation, in ancestor worship, or in the soul's escape to a spiritual realm. Some believe that after death the soul simply fades into the vast expanse of the universe. The other Abrahamic faiths of Judaism and Islam also teach about a bodily resurrection, but in these faiths it is not the core concern that it is in Christianity.

Those of us who live in Christian cultures, conditioned to the celebration of Easter year in and year out, often forget just how strange an idea the resurrection really is. In the Roman Empire of the fourth century, most pagan philosophers and religious leaders found completely absurd the idea that a body could be raised from the dead and live eternally. In his writings St. Augustine defended Christianity against these pagans who said that the body should be escaped at death, not renewed and revived.

Augustine argued that the body "must be cherished" in any authentic Christian faith. He imagined pagans scoffing: "But what of disabilities, disease, distortions of the body?" He answered that our resurrected bodies would be whole and harmonious. Like Jesus's resurrected body, they would bear the scars of the sufferings that shaped us into saints: "a badge of honour, and the beauty of their virtue—a beauty which is in the body, but not of the body—will shine forth in it."[28] That is one of the most remarkable things about the stories of the resurrected Christ: in the accounts of his risen body he still has his wounds, even after he has been resurrected and has ascended to the right hand of God.

"After death comes resurrection," Father Ed reminded me. But hope comes out of loss; in order to rise, you first have to die. In the face of death we often look for a way out, an alternative salvation that doesn't require scars and tombs or waiting for the words "Talitha koum": *Get up!* We put our hope in children, burdening them with the job of creating a better life and better world. We try to insulate our bodies from death and decay. This is the dark side of exercise and fitness—an attempted avoidance of death and a hope of secular resurrection. *If only we hit on the right food, the right mix of supplements and vitamins, the right regimen of strength training and aerobics,* we imagine, *death will pass us by.* Our bodies don't bear out such hopes.

Though I didn't plan it this way, I have lived much of my adult life near a hospital or nursing home. This means that when I run I often pass reminders of death and disease and decay. I am regularly reminded that this body is fragile. My brain could be injured by a wrong landing after a trip on the sidewalk; my heart could reveal a defect in the middle of a race, as happens to otherwise-healthy athletes every year. Fitness is no protection against a car crash.

Rather than insulating us from death, every good workout helps to prepare us for it. The aches and pains and difficulties of the body remind us that we are mortal. Training for sports is training for death. We say "no" to another half hour spent in bed; we lace up our shoes and head out the door. Only after these many small deaths does the grace of a good run or ride come. If we pay attention, these workouts teach us that we are not the source of our own lives.

And so death moves to life; the dark of Good Friday gives way to the light of Easter. This is where Holy Week ends—and Lent, with it—late on Holy Saturday, with everyone gathered together in the darkness. In the back of the church a fire is set; a large, flaming bowl throws shadows across the room. The priest prays over it:

"Sanctify this new fire, and grant that in this paschal feast we may so burn with heavenly desires, that with pure minds we may attain to the festival of everlasting light..."

With an "Amen" the priest lights the Easter candle from the bowl of fire and passes it around; from it, individual congregants light their own candles. Each person holds a fraction of the fire that lights up the world. In the glow of this light we listen together to the whole story of God's redemptive work, from the creation of the world to the call of Abraham, the Exodus of Israel, and Ezekiel's vision of God raising the dead of Israel from a valley of dry bones. We pray, "Let the whole world see and know that things which were cast down are being raised up, and things which had grown old are being made new, and that all things are being brought to their perfection by him through whom all things were made."

This is the night when new Christians are welcomed into the church. Baptisms are performed during the service, the new Christians welcomed with water. In the baptismal blessing all those who have already been baptized, who have already died and risen from those symbolic waters, audibly reaffirm their vows to resist evil, to break bread, and to seek and serve Christ in all persons.

Then there is resurrection. "Alleluia, Christ is risen!" the priest proclaims and the congregation responds, "The Lord is risen indeed. Alleluia!" The light of the paschal candle is brought to the altar and the priest prays: "O God, who made this most holy night to shine with the glory of the Lord's resurrection: Stir up in your Church that Spirit of adoption which is given to us in Baptism, that we, renewed both in body and mind, may worship you in sincerity and truth."

This is resurrection: body and mind, soul and spirit. This is what I was ready for after my long season of Lent, the community of Maundy Thursday, and the mourning of Good Friday. Now it was time to be "renewed both in body and mind." As I left that Easter Vigil celebrating the resurrection of Christ, I turned to my own renewal and resurrection. It would come, this life after death, through a friendship that would grow to affection and lead to love without condition.

———

"Who is Emily Hardin?" I asked Nathanael after hearing her name a few times. She and I had several mutual friends, and I'd hear her name often, but I couldn't remember ever meeting Emily.

"She's the girl you were sitting next to in church!" Nathanael was incredulous that I could be so introverted I hadn't met a person I'd seen nearly every Sunday for months. Emily sat in the same section of church that I did, often alone but sometimes with friends. She had a slender swimmer's body and thick blond hair that she often wore in two braids. She expressed her happy nature as much with her blue-gray eyes as she did with her ready smile. There was a transparency about her, her emotions always clear. We had done nothing more than pass the "Peace of Christ," but even in those moments I saw that she radiated joy.

A couple of months later I approached Father Ed about starting a young adults' group at the church. "Emily Hardin is interested in starting one. You should talk to her," he told me. I called one night from the echoing living room of my nearly empty duplex; Emily was making the five-hour drive to Nashville to visit her sister. In her confident voice, with its strong south Arkansas twang, she spoke of God with the familiarity that comes with having spent much time in prayer. But she didn't want this group to be a gathering of insiders; she wanted to gather a group that would be welcoming to everyone, whether actively seeking God or not.

And so Emily and I began our friendship as co-leaders of the St. Michael's young adults' group. We were often the only ones to show up for the meetings at my duplex; its broad, shaded porch the perfect place to hold summer evening conversations. We drank gin and tonics as cicadas buzzed in the century-old oaks that had buckled and cracked the concrete sidewalks in front of the house. It was easy for us to let the summer nights run on, our conversations lasting beyond what might have been wise for a weeknight. Our subjects ranged from church to theology to our desires to heal the world. We talked about experiences we'd had abroad and our hopes, which had, at this point in our lives, become more open-ended for each of us. Having experienced disappointments and dissatisfactions with our attempts to find happiness, we both were beginning to see happiness as a gift and not as something to be achieved. We were listening.

I noticed a kind of joy in Emily's body; she loved to move, to dance, to swim and hike and do Pilates. She did none of this out of an anxiety about staying fit and in shape. Exercise was never a chore to check off a list for her; it was something she found nourishing and necessary. To swim, for Emily, is to pray with her body; it is a kind of meditation, and she needs it in the same way that many people need to walk. She told me about the time she set out to find a pool in Kenya. She'd been staying in a rural village and hadn't been able to swim in months. She longed for the water desperately, needing it after a time of witnessing suffering on a scale she'd never seen before. When she heard a rumor that there was a pool several hours away from where she was staying, she hired a motorcycle taxi to take her all those miles on rough unpaved roads. She found relief and renewal for her body and soul in the run-down pool of an old colonial hotel. In that story I saw Emily's desire for adventure, willingness to take risks, and need for peace—all signs of her depth.

Emily carried joy in her body, but she also struggled with its betrayals. She'd had a lifelong struggle with Marfan syndrome and all the miseries that come with it. This was a disease that could mean, at its worst, a split in her aorta and sudden death, a possibility she had to watch for and try to prevent by getting annual echocardiograms.

She also struggled off and on throughout life with serious bouts of acne that disappeared for years then appeared again, unexplained and unexpected. I appreciated her perspective on it all. As she said to me once, "Health is a matter of our spirits as much as it is of our bodies, but only the health of our spirits really lasts." Emily exhibited a health that radiated outward and reflected her inward strength.

Through Emily's approach to health—a simple love for the movement and exertion of her body—I came to see that health didn't have to be a struggle. Until that point I was still lost in the attitude that I was fighting a battle with my body. I thought that health required beating my body into submission, not feeling enraptured with the pleasure of its goodness. But in Emily's talk of swimming and Pilates and in her love of long backpacking trips, I saw health in all of its radiant pleasure—something deeper than my binges on cigarettes and Red Bull and convenience-store pizza had ever brought me.

The difference between Emily's longings for the pool and my longings for another Camel Light was in the way our desires had been trained, what we had learned to savor. The problem of "junk food," whether spiritual or physical, is a problem of taste. A Big Mac tastes good to those who don't know any better. But once your taste buds acclimate to real food—good burgers made from grass-fed beef, seasoned well and cooked with care—a Big Mac will become inedible. Smoking a cigarette is superior to taking a run only for those who have never experienced the joy of a run.

To get to this point, entropy must be overcome. This is where the *will* comes in. Kale doesn't taste better than a Big Mac if you just decide to start eating it one day. To retrain our desires we have to go through training periods in which we use our force of will to eat only what is good and avoid what is bad. Go for twenty-one days without eating junk food. Instead, eat real, whole, unprocessed food, seasoned well. After those three weeks a Coke will taste disgustingly sweet, and you won't be able to stomach a fast-food burger.

I am convinced that whatever is healthiest, whatever is best for us, will always be the most pleasurable. Becoming healthy is really a process of learning to enjoy what is truly pleasurable. Christianity is a hedonistic religion in this regard. But hedonism, too, requires discipline. G. K. Chesterton, in *Twelve Types,* put it this way: "The fact is that this purification and austerity are even more necessary for the appreciation of life and laughter than for anything else. To let no bird fly past unnoticed, to spell patiently the stones and weeds, to have the mind a storehouse of sunsets, requires a discipline in pleasure and an education in gratitude."[29]

That Easter season, using Emily as my example, I began to train into the discipline of pleasure. This started with running and with a vision of what running could be. I'd listened to an interview with Christopher McDougall in which he talked about his book *Born to Run,* and I'd been fascinated. Emily gave me the book for my birthday. From McDougall I learned that running should be as natural to my body as walking. My problem was that I had long lived a life of unnatural habits, from shoes to diet, that kept me from enjoying my runs in the way the Tarahumara Indians do in the desert canyons of northern Mexico. These Indians run the equivalent of ultramarathons on a regular basis, wearing nothing more than homemade sandals.

I bought a pair of thin-soled shoes and started to find my way to running in a natural way. I read websites, watched videos, and obsessively studied natural running techniques. With time I found my stride on the roads. My cigarettes started to come at longer and longer intervals. I would go days without one and, when I did have one, would soon regret it after I started a run. My desires were changing, and as they did I was becoming healthier. A joyful resurrection was beginning in my body.

Like Emily, I found myself drawn to distance, and as my body became healthier I began going on long hikes in the woods. I knew of a trail that picked up just outside of Little Rock and decided to hike the length of it with a friend. Emily and some other friends met us toward the end of the trail for camping and an open-fire feast.

I hardly knew what I was doing when we started out, but my friend Jaman and I ended up pushing through twenty miles that day. At the end of that hike, my legs were tired but I felt a kind of sweaty elation I'd never experienced before. Walking a long distance in the woods felt like the purpose for which my body was made; my mind felt sharp and the whole of me was alive. I wanted health, I wanted this goodness in my body, and I was finally ready to leave behind the half pleasures I'd been holding on to for so long.

We camped that night and, after everyone else had retired to tents and sleeping bags, Emily and I stayed up talking and sipping cheap Australian wine. The stars were barely visible through the trees, so we decided to walk together to the road, where a thin strip of sky was clear. Overhead the stars were so bright we could see everything around us, their brightness undiluted by city lights. We lay down on the country road, side by side, and our hands brushed with the kind of electricity that comes from the combination of wine and woods and stars. We found each other's fingers, clasped our hands together in the unmistakable expression of love, and gazed up. In the quiet we could hear our breath, in and out, an exchange of life.

6 Weeks to Ironman

5:40 a.m.

Jim Dailey Fitness & Aquatic Center, Little Rock, Arkansas

My eyes are still crusty with sleep as I pull my goggles on. They're the Swedish kind: two small, hard plastic cups with no rubber or sponge. It is 5:40 a.m. The gym opened ten minutes ago. I have to be at work at 7:45. This hour before sunrise is the only time I have, so I take it.

There is something peaceful about entering the day with an open lap lane and the smell of chlorine and water. I ease my body in. The water is cool. On the concrete lip of the pool I organize my stuff: a couple of hand paddles, a pull buoy, a kickboard, a note card with my workout written on it in pencil. *Fifteen-minute warm up. 4 x 25 pull. 5 x 50 hard. 4 x 250 Zone 3. Kick and cool down.* As I warm up I try to move with my head relaxed, my arms leading, my body streamlined. *Reach for the end,* I tell myself. *Belly to the wall.* I duck and twist to flip over at the end of the lane; the turn I learned in middle school is still easy to recall after repeating it thousands of times in my life.

I gave up swimming for over a decade, never entering a pool for even a recreational lap. It was partly a matter of burnout—too many competitive pressures too early on in my swimming life. It was also because of the way my body was exposed in swimming, nearly naked in a skintight suit. I hated the routine of changing in locker rooms, always feeling a little jealous of those who could change, unashamed, in front of others. Shortly before my middle-school swimming days ended, another swimmer—lean and strong, Olympic material some said —had made fun of my butt. As I waited my turn for a drill, he stood behind me, pointing my butt out to other boys and pretending to run up and kick it as I bent over before a dive. I pretended to ignore him at the time but felt once more that my body didn't fit this sport.

Now I'm back in the pool again. No one is around this early except for one still-waking lifeguard, an old man who's water running, and another swimmer wholly absorbed in his own laps. I no longer feel self-conscious to have my body exposed in the water. There is no use in worrying about it anymore. This is my body, for better or worse. It is what I have to work with, and now I am working with it. I am training these arms and legs and shoulders, this stomach and this neck, for the day when I will have to move my self in its entirety, all my parts bodily and spiritual, to a finish line that stands 140.6 miles in the distance.

I practice for the initial surge of the race, when I will have to crawl through hundreds of bodies to find open water. I sprint hard, imagining the crowd in the wide ocean. And then it's on to endurance, my heart beating steady and hard in the quiet of the water. I push through two hundred fifty meters, ten laps, swimming hard but balancing my effort with the distance. My body feels both mechanical and alive, each stroke placed with precision.

Swimming is a technical sport, a test of much more than fitness. To swim well is to know how to move your body in water. It is like dance. Muscle is gained, aerobic capacity earned, in service of sharpening the body's precision. In its emphasis on focus and concentration, swimming is also like yoga. There is something in the body that longs to be focused, that appreciates the precision of movement our varied muscles afford us. I know that my workout is finished when my form falls apart and my body can no longer move smoothly through the water. Then it's time for a cool down with easy laps, sometimes sloppy. I grab a foam board and kick a couple of laps up and down the lane.

The locker room fills up as I strip off my skintight jammers and rinse chlorine off my body in the open showers. There are young and old in the room, fat and thin, people of all skin colors. Some are muscled but most are here to shed the inevitable pounds collected in a normal American life. I no longer feel ashamed of my body in a locker room, not because I feel fit and strong, but because I have to accept that this is my body. There is no sense in wanting something else; my body is what it is. The healthy response is to accept and glory in its blessings as much as in its failures. To train and race is to live in my body's joy.

This Is My
Beloved Body

I remember the sweat stains I left on the floor that summer from the bicycle crunches, the woodchoppers, the Russian high jumps, and other functional exercises Lorrie had planned out in two alternating circuits. My progress was slow, but my body was becoming fitter—the weights easier to push, my muscles less sore after each repetition. But more important than my increasing fitness was the way my relationship to exercise was changing. I had started working out in an effort to prove something to Liz, but I hadn't succeeded in becoming much healthier. Now, under the influence of Emily's love, I was living into my body as subject rather than object. Emily loved my body because it was mine. Her love for me was whole and unfractured; it called me to be whole in response.

To put the word *love* in front of something can make it sound sappy and cliché, and perhaps it is cliché to say that love makes people whole. But this statement is also true in a way deeper than the much-abused word *love* can convey. Emily's wholehearted embrace of me led me to turn my life away from the emptiness of junk food and cigarettes. She lived into the best definition of love: she wanted, wholly and unselfishly, all that was best for me.

From Emily I learned not only how to enjoy the movement of my body in exercise but also how to train. Emily loved going long, whether that meant backpacking the two hundred miles of the arduous Ozark Highlands Trail or swimming for hours in a secluded mountain lake. During the first autumn of our relationship, Emily signed up for a challenge beyond anything she'd accomplished to that point: a 12.5-mile swim around the island of Key West.

Watching her daily swims and her long, weekend training sessions at a hidden lake in the Ouachita Mountains known only by locals renewed in me a desire to race a triathlon. I'd been curious about the sport since I was in college and first saw coverage of the Ironman on television. It seemed to me the ultimate expression of fitness and was far more interesting than setting out to race a 5K or a marathon. There was something about triathlon that appealed to my natural "go big or go home" tendencies. So soon after Emily signed up for her swim, I signed up for my first triathlon—a sprint distance race, to be held that spring.

After that, the focus of my workouts changed from exercising in order to get fit, to training for a race. "Exercise" had been an act of moving toward some abstract idea of health; "training" meant working my body toward a specific goal. In training I found a reason for every movement; each was aimed at getting me through the swim and bike ride and run of a specific, future race day. I borrowed a bike from Emily and started riding. I swam a couple of times a week at the local rec center. I put more purpose into my running, focusing my attention on building my distance up to the 5K I'd have to run after the bike portion of the race.

My body was still at least fifty pounds overweight, so each training session was like biking and running while wearing a weighted vest. On top of that, the details of actually racing and not just training for a triathlon suddenly seemed impossibly technical. I had no idea how to switch from the swim to the bike to the run. Would I change clothes in between? Should I wear my running shoes on the bike? To help, Emily gave me a beginner's triathlon book, and I obsessively started researching the sport, reading everything from *Triathlete* magazine to the forums on triathlon websites. My desire to race grew, but my sense of readiness didn't.

Fear of failure came over me. I wasn't ready. I e-mailed the race organizers and made up an excuse about why I couldn't come. In a kind of grace rarely exhibited among race producers, the director wrote back, "No problem. We would be glad to transfer your registration to another triathlon later in the season." I punted my deadline for race readiness to August. I had to keep on training.

Emily continued preparing for her race. Whatever fear she felt about her swim didn't stop her from getting on that plane to Florida. We flew together, met up with her sister Sally in Fort Lauderdale, then drove down US 1—past alligators and crab shacks, kitsch stores and ocean theme parks—to the point where the nation drops into the Gulf. The host hotel held registration by its poolside tiki bar. Then came a sleepless night as we tried to rest up for the work ahead.

As the pilot crew, Sally and I would kayak alongside Emily as she swam. It was our job to keep Emily on course, give her food and water, and make sure passing boats saw her. Emily had to swim the 12.5 miles around the island of Key West without ever standing or holding onto the boat. If she stopped for food, water, or a bathroom break, she had to tread water or float. Despite all the training she'd done, we hadn't practiced any of these logistics.

Sunlight cracked a pink line on the ocean horizon as we drove to Smathers Beach. The fifty-some swimmers were pulling up, car by car, their pilots helping them get ready for the day. Regular sunscreen isn't up to the challenge of protecting swimmers throughout an eight-hour ocean swim, so all of the racers were smearing themselves with thick layers of white zinc oxide, making their bodies appear ghostlike. A missed spot could mean a blistering burn.

Once our rented kayak was delivered, we were ready. There was a final briefing for swimmers and pilots, then the swimmers gathered in the water behind the start buoys. Sally and I ran our kayak into the ocean and paddled out with the other pilots. A bullhorn blew from the race official's boat, and the pilots started paddling. The waves were high and choppy. From time to time a swimmer appeared behind a swell, then disappeared again. We'd painted Emily's swim cap to make her easier to recognize in the crowd, but in the vastness of the water those small markings now seemed inadequate. It was hard to tell one swimmer from another. Finally we saw her, coming up just past the race official's boat. Sally and I paddled hard to meet her.

The rough start was making Emily feel desperate. No Arkansas lake had waves like these; the heavy taste of salt hadn't been an issue there as it was here. But the rough waters didn't last long.

"It's clear up ahead!" I yelled to Emily as we quickly neared a turn that would take her around the island. After that turn the waters were calm. It took us an hour to sort out our rhythm—which side of the kayak Emily would swim on, how to pass water back and forth. We were clearly amateurs at this, with our rope-tethered Nalgene water bottle that took in seawater as we threw it to Emily.

After the first few hours our paddle strokes and swim strokes moved in a rhythm. We occasionally saw another swimmer and pilot boat. Some swimmers were even accompanied by party barges that held a crew of friends and relatives who rooted them along. Most were followed by a single kayaker: a husband or wife or friend. In areas of heavy traffic, we watched carefully for boats that threatened to come too close. In calm waters we drifted along, watching the shoreline. We saw big brown pelicans standing on the piers with their heads down—icons of the Gulf. Frigate birds with their kite-like wings, too long for any land bird, circled overhead like ancient surveyors and guides. Weathered fishermen stood on the shore with five-gallon buckets. We scanned the horizon for dolphins.

When we passed our hotel on the opposite side of the island and crossed under the bridge for Highway 1, I knew that we had made it well over halfway. Emily had been swimming strong and steady for hours, but she hadn't felt like eating much and had taken in only a few handfuls of electrolyte jellybeans over the five hours she'd been swimming. The crash came as we moved under the bridge and into shallow waters. The tide was going out, and the waters we were now moving through were full of seaweed and sandbars that made swimming difficult. The water was so shallow in places, Emily had to do the breaststroke just to move through the water at all. Swimming the breaststroke rather than the traditional freestyle stroke meant she was expending more energy. Needing to do this was a possibility for which she hadn't prepared.

Emily struggled forward, more slowly now. I could see Smathers Beach, location of the finish line, on the horizon. But Emily's glycogen stores were empty, her body unable to move forward. A cascade of sodium and blood sugar imbalances were sending her into a kind of delirious exhaustion. We stopped the kayak and she lay on her back, floating in the shallow water, crying from exhaustion.

"Just stand up. Stand up!" Sally yelled at her from the boat, worried about her sister lying in the ocean, physically and emotionally drained. But Emily wouldn't stand up. For all her lack of energy, she still had a will to finish. Finishing was more important than any win. She had come to swim around Key West and that was what she would do—no shortcuts, no asterisks after her name on the list of finishers.

The finish is the moment of truth of any endurance race. Whether one pushes toward that line, giving all of one's body and soul to the effort, or instead gives up, is a measure of one's character. Sometimes because of health or cutoff times a good athlete won't reach the finish line, but that is a reality that must be accepted only after one has given one's all.

American Chris Lieto demonstrated this character of a finisher after his lead in the 2011 Ironman World Championship evaporated; his body couldn't keep up the pace. Unlike the many pros who quit after a place on the podium ceases to be an option, he pushed through, slowly jogging and walking to the end. Finishing was also the moment of truth at the Kona Ironman in 1982 when Julie Moss stumbled and fell—and eventually crawled across the finish line, a moment that was broadcast on ABC's *Wide World of Sports*. Many athletes, from amateurs to professionals, name her act of determination and endurance as their inspiration for starting their pursuit of triathlon. To go long is to focus one's whole self on finishing.

Emily could have stood at that moment; no one else would have known. But she had come to swim the whole distance and that was what she was going to do. I jumped out of the boat and waded through the water to where Emily was floating on her back. I gave her a handful of sports beans that she ate hungrily, and I poured water into her mouth.

"Less than a mile to go," I said, not really knowing if that was the case. "I can see the finish line," I lied. "I love you so much and you can do this." This I said with all I knew to be true. The sugar entered her blood stream quickly; the fresh water quenched her thirst.

"Let's go," Emily said with tired determination.

We worked to move into deeper water and we found it. Emily swam her long, beautiful stroke, and my lie became a truth. The finish line appeared on the horizon. We heard the music. Whether running a 5K or a marathon or swimming a race like this one, whatever music is played at the finish line is the best music a racer has ever heard. There was no reason to hold back or save energy now. Emily gave her all to cover the final distance.

We passed through buoys that marked the finish line and moved toward the shore. The water was shallow, and we called to Emily, "You finished! You finished!"

"Are you sure?" Emily answered in disbelief, not wanting to stand until she was certain.

"Yes!" we said. "Stand up!" Emily stood after having spent eight hours in the ocean: twelve and a half miles of swimming. She waded up to the beach, shaking from an equal mix of joy and low blood sugar. We hungrily ate hot dogs from the grill. A race organizer hung a finisher's medal around Emily's neck. She was the last to finish that day, the last to make it all the way without stopping or standing.

That evening—our sunburned bodies freshly showered, fresh clothes over our tired muscles—we ate oysters and Key lime pie on a wharf we had passed hours before. We would leave in the morning. Our work in Key West was finished—or almost finished.

"Let's go sit on the beach at sunset," I said to Emily. We went back to the shoreline where her swim had started and ended. We sat on the sand, looking out at the ocean that seemed pregnant with life and possibility and mystery. I began to recite all of the things I loved about her and what she had meant to me over the last months, and she answered in the same way. Then, the ocean all around us, our bodies exhausted but exhilarated, I knelt on the sand and pulled a ring from my pocket.

"Will you marry me?" I asked. She said yes, and together we said yes to the time and beauty, the growth and joy, the pain and hope that lay ahead.

It took those hours spent in the kayak, paddling alongside Emily, to get me to the starting line of my first triathlon. Seeing her effort and exhaustion, but also her joy, made me want to experience the same thing myself. Other than the occasional middle-school swim meet, I'd never raced anything: no 5Ks or fun runs, no bike races or distance swims. Watching Emily, I'd finally grasped the thrill of racing, and I knew better now what I needed to do to get to race day.

My haphazard triathlon training through the spring had taught me what was required to train for a triathlon, and I knew that I needed a firm plan that I could follow, day in and day out. I searched the Internet for "beginner + sprint + triathlon + plan" and sorted through the top results. One plan that included workouts for each day laid out on a calendar looked simple and easy to understand. I became obedient to that plan, following it like a monastic rule of life, rising each day to run or bike or swim for however long that piece of paper told me to. If it said to run hills on one day, I went to the best hill I knew and ran up and down it. If it told me to ride hard, I pedaled my heavy old bike along a bike path until the sweat poured from under my helmet. I also rested when the plan called on me to rest, and in this I found the balance that leads to strength.

I read triathlon magazines and books. I watched training videos and race highlights. I hung out in bike shops and picked up the language of triathlon and cycling. I learned bike gear ratios and what a clipless pedal was and how aerobars help the body cut through the air. I learned that a bike-to-run workout is called a "brick" and that I was a "newbie." I entered and became a part of a new culture and its form of life. I started to know the kinds of things runners know and cyclists know. Before training I'd never heard of a hip flexor. I'd known only vaguely where my Achilles tendon could be found. Now I started to learn the names of those body parts that were becoming sore in the process of strengthening them. In learning this language and entering this life, I was also saying good-bye to a life of cigarettes and junk food; these were realities that didn't make sense in the life of a triathlete, and that's what I was becoming.

I was becoming a triathlete, not only because I was trying to lose weight but because I'd stuck with the sport long enough to love it and, as with any love, I wanted to spend more and more of my time with it. For too many people, exercise is an unpleasant pill to be swallowed. It's an "Eat your spinach" mentality: do something good but unpleasant. Here is what I've discovered: If your spinach doesn't taste delicious, then you need to find a new recipe. Similarly, if your workouts aren't life-giving, then it's time try something else.

Most people give up on exercise because they never learn to love a sport. Exercise becomes an economic exchange of work and calories and nothing more. I don't care anymore about how many calories I burn. What matters at the end of my workout is whether it has made me go longer or faster or stronger. I haven't "exercised" in years, but I train almost every day. Some race or goal is always on my calendar. I have to be ready.

When I started into my final week of training in August, I was finally ready to race. I knew that I could finish and that was all I wanted: to make it through the swim and bike and run. Those imagined distances started to take on form for me when Emily and I drove down to the race site, her old, red road bike strapped on to her rickety bike rack. We arrived the day before the race to register and drive the course. I checked in at the big tents that had been set up in the parking lot and went through the routine that would soon become familiar to me: collecting my race numbers and timing chip, my T-shirt and swag bag.

I looked around the transition area. There were long rows of A-frame bike racks where athletes would hang their bikes during the race.

On either side of the staging area there were "Run Out" and "Bike Out" signs posted to save the confused athlete come race day. Emily and I walked down to the water and looked out over the distance marked by the buoys; I visualized myself making the turn around them. As we drove the bike course, I imagined how the hills' inclines, now obscured by the horsepower of the car's engine, would feel under my bike. We followed the run course with its forgiving downhill to the finish line. I was ready with an energy I hadn't felt in years. I felt like a raging bull in a rodeo chute, my body longing for release after years of confining limits.

We arrived early on race morning, the sky still dark even in those longest days of summer. Only a few other racers had pulled into the grassy field designated for parking; headlamps strapped to foreheads bobbed in the distance as athletes walked their bikes to the transition area. I went through my checklist: rack my bike; lay out my towel, shoes, helmet, and sunglasses. Next came the body marking that was conducted by a team of volunteers armed with Sharpies: my race number was written on my arms; my age, "30," on the back of my leg. I strapped my timing chip to my left ankle, where it wouldn't catch on the gears of the bike. I was ready with an hour to spare.

Emily and I walked down to the lake's edge, near the swim's starting point. I was filled with a nervous energy that I'd never felt before, my stomach uneasy as athletes arrived by the hundreds and the sun rose. I went back to my transition area again and again, constantly rearranging my gear to match the order being used by racers who looked like they knew what they were doing. I switched my bike from hanging by its handlebars to hanging by its seat, then switched it back again. Mercifully, the transition area was finally closed to racers and I couldn't rearrange anymore.

I looked out over the water and listened in a daze as someone sang the national anthem. The race director—a preacher on the weekends when he's not running triathlons—offered a prayer. Finally the athletes were called to enter the water. I was in the first wave, along with the other men under forty. I kissed Emily and hugged my parents, who had joined us just before the race start. After that, I was on my own until the finish line.

The athletes—thin and fat, fit and getting there—gathered in a mass in the water. We arranged ourselves behind the start buoys. My goals for the swim were simple: to survive and to not get kicked in the face. This wasn't going to be a fast swim, but I hoped it would be a safe one.

Then the horn sounded and there was no more time for thinking. Arms and legs flailed in the water. I pushed into the chaos, pointing my body toward the buoy on the horizon. *Stroke, breath...stroke, breath... stroke, breath... Look for the buoy and then down again.* I became locked in a feeling of presence I'd never experienced before. I arrived at the shore, lined with cheering friends and relatives, faster than I expected. I ran from the water and saw Emily standing nearby.

"You can do it, babe!" she called. "Go, go!"

And I went, pushing hard on my bike pedals up and down the lakeside hills. I was passed often, but I also passed a few riders. The intensity and the effort of concentrating my body on every moment kept me centered in a time that felt outside of time. Einstein's theory of relativity does not feel theoretical or mysterious to an athlete. I was entering the addictive "flow" of absolute presence.

By the run portion of the race I was soaked with sweat, my body pouring out salt and water in a useless effort to cool me in the August heat. At the water stations I copied the experienced runners ahead of me, drinking water and dropping ice down my shirt—one cup for the inside of me, a second cup for the outside. In the end, I found that I couldn't run the whole of the 5K, but I did my best, walking the hills till my pounding heart calmed enough for me to start running again.

The course was out and back, a long hill up followed by a long return back down. I ran the whole way back, my side hurting, but the sound of the finish line giving me reason to focus not on worrying but on finishing.

When I got near I gave my all to running, sprinting with every bit of energy I had left. I could see Emily and my parents beyond the finish gate. I rushed toward it, feeling a joy in my body I hadn't felt since I was a kid running down a hill with a cape flying behind me, wondering if I could fly if I got up enough speed.

And then the race was over: my body exhausted, my heart still racing, every bit of me soaked with sweat. I had finished. I had run this race to the end, and even though I trailed the winner by nearly an hour, it felt like I'd just won. I *had* won, against the inertia of myself. I had trained and raced and felt my body begin its journey on a path of rebirth.

I was practicing for resurrection.

4 Weeks to Ironman

7:30 a.m.
Ferndale, Arkansas

Roger Weldon is a banker with a big corner office. He's also a sage of sorts who regularly posts epicurean aphorisms on Facebook. He seeks and shares the good life—a life he finds in faith and family and in going really fast. He's a man of seeming contradictions: a well-read vegetarian with a gun collection that would make any NRA member proud. He's a man who savors, and what he seems to savor most of all is showing young men, sometimes twenty years his junior, that he can go faster than they can. After that, he likes to show them how *they* can get faster.

Any ride with Roger at the lead was a ride that revealed to me new things about myself. Any weakness, a cold coming on, any vulnerable point in my training would be spotlighted by mile twenty. A compliment from Roger, though he was never stingy with them, meant more to me than a kind word from almost anyone else. "Looking strong on those hills, Ragan," he'd call out as he circled past me to the front of the pack, and I'd feel glad for all the heavy squatting I'd been doing.

For Roger, Ironman, triathlon, and riding hard were means of personal discovery. Triathlon was a kind of heuristic tool, a way to find out about himself and his deepest dependencies. Like the Desert Fathers and Mothers, who subjected their bodies to extremes of fasting and sleeplessness and exposure, Roger pursued hard physical discipline and work for reasons greater than spiritual spectacle. Bodily deprivation and disciplines were tools that could reveal the unresolved lack in the self: stubborn kernels of sin and selfishness that went undetected in the less extreme routines of the day-to-day.

Roger led rides not in the role of coach but as a kind of spiritual master, like the Abbas of old who trained young monks into the ways of God. Unresolved individual issues came up during rides with Roger because he had done the hard work it took to arrive first at the finish line, and he was ready to show others how we too could shed our slow, unwieldy spirits and achieve that vision. If I have one regret about training for the Ironman, it is that I didn't spend more time training with Roger Weldon.

This particular morning we arrive by dawn. We're a regular crew: most of us are very fast; a few, like me, can barely keep up. "Let's ride," Roger says. There's the familiar cascade of clicks—shoes locking into bike pedals, men and women becoming one with their machines. We pass fields and peri-urban estates as we ride in the gold light of a cool fall morning. We pedal, spinning easily at first to warm up. Then it's on: single-file drafting, one after the other, switching off who's in the front. I have to work to hang on, but as long as I stay on the wheel of the rider ahead of me, it's possible for me to keep with the pack, even at speeds that creep past twenty-five miles per hour.

Then it's my turn to lead. There's no one else to cut a path through the wind, but I can't let down the pace. I push with everything in me, pulling the others along, pushing my heart rate into the red of Zone 5. None of us except maybe Roger could keep up the speeds we're traveling if we had to lead the whole way. That's the point of a group: working together on the road, switching off at the front like a flock of geese taking turns at the point of their V. After a while everything starts to feel fast and focused; it's easy to be lulled into the rhythm of the ride. Then the hills come and everything goes to pieces. The stronger riders can keep up the pace, pushing through the hills. Those of us who aren't as strong drop, one by one, forming our own little packs or, worse, riding solo for miles.

On a particularly long hill I am dropped, the pack moving far ahead. I don't think they're catchable, even with a hard push. Just after I crest the hill, another rider comes up beside me. It is Jeff Glasbrenner, something of a local legend. Jeff is a semipro triathlete who completed a dozen Ironman triathlons not in a lifetime but in one year. He's done all this despite having only one leg, a reality he accepts as a fact rather than a mere limit.

"Let's work together and go catch them," Jeff says. We hit it, each pulling a minute on and a minute off, switching off which one of us rides in front, the other drafting closely behind. With hard work we are topping speeds of well over twenty-six miles per hour. It isn't enough for us to catch the group; they're already too far ahead. But it gives me a chance to see a real athlete at work, pushing his body at respectable speeds even without use of the additional muscles available to other racers.

What I learned from watching Jeff and others in triathlon is a frank acceptance of my body and its limits. There are people who naturally have the gifts of speed and those who don't. There are men and women who are just faster than me and will always be faster, no matter how much training I do. In training, what matters is what you do with your body—with the mix of muscles and oxygen capacity you alone were given. Whatever limits you have—a leg missing, a tendency toward fat, flat feet—those are the facts of your body. The question is, what do you do with those limits? How will you dance with them and around them? Jeff uses good prosthetics and trains his body to be the best it can be, and that best is really fast.

My own limit was my weight, a weight that began to slip away as I accepted the reality of myself—that while others can eat carbs freely, I have to limit them to the extreme. That is the fact of my body. If I am to live into the fullness of that fact, I have to limit my intake of carbs.

I also have the happily chosen limit of a family life and the responsibility of love, which keeps me from training three hours a day, every day. I have to accept the limits that love places upon me, in order to train in a way that prepares me as best as those limits of love and health will allow. This is how we become better, by accepting the limits of ourselves and by living within those limits, not beyond them. This doesn't mean that we don't test the boundary lines, or that we don't recognize our tendencies to keep ourselves from our full potential. But we have to live into the reality of our selves. We must live into our glory but also live within the borders that give each self a meaningful shape.

Life lived beyond limits is like cancer—a disease in which cells don't know when to stop growing and continue beyond the boundaries of health. Limits are not bars on a cage; limits are an invitation to live more deeply in our bodies and lives. When we accept that there is only so much work we can do before we have to stop and rest and trust in God, then we can live into a kind of Sabbath life. A good coach will tell you that stress followed by rest is how real improvement happens. Denying the limits of the body leads to a serious problem known as overtraining, in which the body can become chronically fatigued for months.

Jeff and I found our group stopped a few miles ahead. Sweat poured down my head and coated my sunglasses with a salty film. Our gaggle of riders now reassembled, we were ready to go again.

The last ten miles of the ride were easier for Jeff and me, with a big group now ahead of us to cut the wind and with most of the real hills behind us. We had met and pushed up against our limits, and that is what you really want from a good morning of training: sore muscles, a hungry stomach, and a relaxing afternoon ahead.

This Is My Given Body

February is a good time to go to the beach, so that is what Emily and I did, flying down to the Caribbean and taking the ferry over to a small island called Nevis. This was our honeymoon, taken a month after the wedding we'd held on a cold January day. We were settling into our life together after all of the welcome exhaustion of celebration and moving and the logistics of bringing two lives together. Now it was time to rest for a week in the island vacation home generously loaned to us by a friend's family. We ate well, hiked, and swam. As chance would have it, the local bike-rental shack was hosting a sprint triathlon that week, and I raced in that too.

Alone, we were free with our bodies, and we lived into the joy for which they are meant. We savored the world—a lobster tail trembling white with butter; fresh hibiscus tea, crimson and sweet; a coconut just split by a machete, the milk cool, its flesh rich and creamy; salt and skin. It was a week of gifts—a week without death and decay or worry about "what ifs" or what life would bring. It was a "palace in time" —Rabbi Abraham Joshua Heschel's phrase for the practice of Sabbath retreat where the world of things fades into a sense of the eternal time of the divine—and in that, it was godlike.

I use the word *godlike* not as sacrilege but as an invitation. Athanasius once said: "He, indeed, assumed humanity that we might become God."[30]

This is the meaning of the incarnation, not a stooping down but a lifting up. We are called to be godlike, and this possibility is ultimately our gift, whatever our limits. For Emily and me, this week of honeymoon Sabbath was a time for us to experience the life of the divinity. The divine life is a life without worry; it is a life all-powerful, all-loving, and all-knowing. We participated in this life, not possessing it, but letting go of ourselves into the flow of God's will. In this we were free, and our lives for a moment seemed to move with, and not against, the grain of the universe.

Free lives are lives that are lived generously, without worry about lack or scarcity. In that freedom, Emily and I gave our bodies readily to one another. It was during that week that Emily became pregnant, and in this way too our lives reflected the divine life. The divine life is a life of community: Father, Son, and Spirit made one through love. And love is always fecund, always ready to include *more* within its embrace. Creation wasn't birthed out of some need for God to have something to glorify God's self. Creation was born because the circle of the Trinity's love expanded as all circles of love must expand: circles that keep on encircling.

As Emily and I settled into life together we also settled into a life of expectation. We tracked the progress of the life inside her using charts that marked the baby's development by weeks—a body bursting forth from latent genetics. Emily's attention to her own body and my attention to her body also changed. With a child inside her, we noticed that the hazards of the world seemed suddenly to loom everywhere. We had always tried to eat locally grown, organic food. We were particularly conscientious about buying meat from local farmers who grazed their animals on grass. But we'd done this out of concern for the health of the earth more than for our own health.

With this new life inside of Emily, we suddenly became aware of how toxic people have made the world in our mad dash for convenience and luxury. Cheap plastics pervert our hormones; pesticides throw our genes into confusion. In the modern world we don't have to wait for natural causes to kill us; our desperate attempts at control ensure that our own meddling will bring about our demise. It seemed a futile task to try to eat healthily, given the far reach of disease in our world. But Emily did what she could, taking fish oil that had the mercury removed, avoiding the shampoos and soaps and sunscreens made with endocrine disrupters.

But the body's troubles don't always originate from the outside. This pregnancy came with risk for Emily as much as for the life inside of her. Emily has a condition called Marfan syndrome. The syndrome is not fully understood, but its basis is genetic and any children we have are born with a 50 percent chance of having it as well. There are mild and extreme forms of the syndrome, and Emily's is mild. Flat feet and a tall, lanky body are the primary markers for her. But this being a disease that affects the connective tissue of the body, there are also risks to the heart. Emily went undiagnosed for most of her life. When her brother learned about Marfan syndrome in medical school, he pointed out that she had many of the features. Her diagnosis was eventually confirmed by a geneticist. Because of her diagnosis of Marfan syndrome, most obstetricians wouldn't take her as a patient. There was a high risk that during the course of the pregnancy, and especially during delivery, her aorta would tear, and this would likely kill her.

We were referred to Dr. Phillips, a high-risk OB who worked at the nearby university hospital. With his straightforward manner and husky frame, he reminded us of a football coach, and we later learned that coaching had indeed been his plan B. With risk and technology come tests and more tests. In the context of a research hospital, the body becomes the subject of study. Small groups of students were present at all of our ultrasounds; they took notes and measured every part of our developing baby. Each measurement seemed to reveal a new potential risk.

"Your baby's heart size is on the high end of average. It's probably nothing, but..."

"There's a white spot on the brain that can sometimes be a marker for Down's, but it will probably go away."

"The baby's urinary tract is blocked. It will probably resolve, but..."

The first few times this happened we left and cried and worried hard, but over time we found that "it could be" was something we couldn't dwell on. There was no use worrying about the "what ifs." There was nothing we could do but welcome this new life and deal with whatever came, whether that was something measurements and sonograms had detected or not.

But those were the issues that concerned the baby; these were not questions of life or death, for the most part. Those questions hung over Emily, but she didn't allow herself to be defined by them. She was full of life and expectation and plans. I was the one who quietly worried, calculating the risks, unable to imagine the potential loss.

The strange truth of human life and human bodies is that although we will not live forever, we can't live as though we are going to die. We make plans even without a guarantee of days in which to fulfill them. This impossibility of living into the reality of our possible deaths speaks to death's absolute alienation from life. In the Christian story death is not natural; it is not a part of the world as the world should be. Death is an aberration, a perversion. The whole Christian story can be seen as a struggle between the systems of Death and the kingdom of Life.

Throughout her pregnancy, Emily lived fully into the life that was hers, one that could be interrupted by death though not ended by it. Her heart seemed fine, perhaps helped along by long walks and daily swims. Her body was, in fact, burgeoning with life, its contours chang-ing, her hips widening and breasts swelling with the miracle of motherhood.

Men's bodies change throughout life but not to the extent that women's bodies do. I imagine that it has been easier for men to be Gnostics, to deny the body's important role in the self, than it has been for women. We do not have to remember our bodies in the same way women must. For women—with hip bones that slip from their sockets and bellies that swell with life, whose monthly bleeding renews the pos-sibility of nurturing life inside—the body is an inevitable concern. Men who do not watch and learn from women are likely to forget what a gift it is to have a body and thus live as though the body doesn't really matter.

Those who work with their hands also help us to remember the truth of our embodiment. For those who end their days with their mus-cles as tired as their minds, it is hard to deny that the body is an integral part of the self. It is upon their physical work—the growing of food, the building of houses, the paving of roads—that our most basic well-being depends. Those in power, who sit at thrones or desks, have always depended upon the work of those who labor with their bodies. The hope of the world dwells upon those bodies: bodies of peasants, fisher-men, women, crucified criminals. Both women and manual laborers share the knowledge that the body, for all of its gifts, is also given to its limits and betrayals. This too is a reality of the embodied life.

One day in early September I got a call from Emily.

"I want you to pray," she said. "I'm having chest pains—I think we should go in." I remember clearly how the sky looked that day as I drove to get her from work: that perfect blue with scattered, white stratus clouds that always marked the transition from summer to fall in Arkansas.

When Emily got in the car she was already on the phone with the nurse. She told us to go straight to the obstetrics ward, where they could check out both Emily's heart and the baby. I felt a deep panic inside. A tear in Emily's aorta would be like a tear down the middle of my self.

A nurse was waiting for us at the obstetrics ward. She ushered us into a small triage center. Emily was stripped down, dressed in a gown, and attached to cords and cables that would help them monitor her heart and the heart of our baby. After an hour and a half, they gave us the all clear. The chest pain was nothing we had to worry about— severe heartburn, most likely. Emily was safe and our baby was safe, and they would stay that way for the last remaining weeks of their lives lived symbiotically, mother and child embodied together.

Against this background of ultrasound anxieties, echocardiograms, and the careful monitoring of brain stems and aortic roots, the beginning of labor arrived calmly and casually several weeks later. It was late November, and we were about to go out for dinner when Emily came into the living room.

"I think my water broke!" she said with a kind of *this-is-happening* bewilderment. We were both filled with a sense of calm. Major contractions hadn't started, and so we did what we were going to do anyway: we ate. We had been told many times that after we entered the obstetrics ward, Emily wouldn't be able to eat. So we ordered takeout from Pei Wei and ate Kung Pao chicken sitting at the empty tables of the hospital's café.

Emily and I felt a Zen-like calm as we made our way up to the obstetrics ward. We had trained for this, and by the end of this labor a new life would be in the world. We were taken to a private birthing room with wood-paneled walls and a broad, tinted glass window that looked out on to the parking lots below. It was dark outside, and I could see cars on the interstate in the distance. The lights were kept low to encourage Emily to sleep. But that was impossible with nurses coming in and out and med students in little packs making their rounds. We watched videos on the Funny or Die website and television shows on Hulu. It felt like Christmas Eve, the anticipation of waiting, the knowing that the next day would bring with it a gift.

The night passed but Emily's labor didn't progress. There was a change of shifts bringing a different nurse and a different anesthesiologist. One nurse gently recommended Pitocin. We agreed, but hours passed, and it became clear that Emily's labor wasn't moving along as quickly as the medical staff wanted.

Dr. Phillips came in. We'd hardly seen him up to that point, but now he was checking in more often. "You're not progressing fast enough," he told Emily. "If we don't see more dilation in the next hour we're going to have to start talking about a C-section." Emily and I had gone into the hospital feeling open to the process; we didn't care one way or another how this baby came into the world as long as it was safe and healthy. But upon hearing this warning, Emily had the desperate realization that she didn't want a C-section; she wanted to give birth naturally. In exhaustion and frustration she began to cry.

Emily's nurse began to work with her, moving Emily into various positions, acting the part of doula. Emily's labor responded, her contractions spiking on the monitor, the spasms moving closer together. What had been mild became strong, and she began to feel real pain. The anesthesiologist came in and tried to adjust the epidural, but it wasn't taking. Because of the risks she faced in labor, Emily had to have an epidural, we'd been told. The prevailing wisdom was that an epidural could help keep Emily's blood pressure low and relieve some of the stress that labor would place on her heart.

The labor started progressing more quickly as we came up on Dr. Phillips's deadline. "You're good," he said after checking Emily. "I don't think we're going to need a C-section." With that he was gone again, and we were left with the nurse and a young medical student who had been awkwardly checking in on us. As the contractions spiked Emily began to be in sharp pain. I held her hand and watched the heart monitor nervously. "We need the anesthesiologist," I told the nurse, but he didn't respond when paged. Finally, another anesthesiologist came and switched out the drugs, and Emily began to feel some relief.

By this time her labor was going full force, and she was pushing hard. Emily wanted her hospital gown off; she wanted her body free. She was possessed suddenly with a wild kind of energy. "Pray," she said with a kind of desperation. "Is everyone praying?" "Yes," we all agreed, none of us daring to say no. A medical student and I held her legs, providing resistance against which she could push. This was the work of the body at its furthest edge. I had been prepared to motivate Emily by saying, "You swam around Key West; you swam 12.5 miles; you can do this!" But I soon saw that this work of endurance was greater than that required by any swim or run or bike ride. Ironman, Tour de France— any woman who has given birth has completed something harder.

Emily was pushing hard, but she was getting tired. Dr. Phillips helped her count slowly to each push. He was calm and confident. "You are going to do it." Emily pushed and pushed hard. "Tell me what you said again," she cried to Dr. Phillips. He told her what Emily had so often told me, the simple words we all need to move forward: "You can do this. You're going to do it." Our daughter's head began to emerge from Emily's body—physical reality, saturated with the holy.

And then our baby was free! Dr. Phillips handed me scissors, and I cut the umbilical cord. Lillian Mae was now living out in the world, independent of Emily's body. I carried her small, crying body to Emily and helped her latch on for her first drink of milk and colostrum. For a moment the staff left the room, and we were alone. I looked at Emily and Lily, huddled together after the common miracle of birth, and recognized the same holy glow depicted in Renaissance paintings of the Madonna and child.

2 Weeks to Ironman

5:00 a.m.
Little Rock, Arkansas

It's early. Emily is still asleep but Lily likes mornings as much as her father does. She kicks her legs, rocking herself in her bouncer seat; plush teddy bear "ears" frame her head. I'm on my bike, which is mounted on a stationary trainer in my home office. Sweat is pouring from my forehead as I push hard through another interval: three minutes, as hard as I can go; three minutes, spinning my legs on an easy gear. Lily seems to like the bike trainer. Whenever she wakes early on days when I need to train, I put her in her bouncy chair next to the bike trainer and push through some intervals. By the time I'm done she usually has been lulled back to sleep by the whir and spin of its wheels.

Lily is nearly one now. In a little over a month she will have her first birthday. In a couple of weeks I will attempt to finish my first Ironman. This Ironman is significant. It will be a major accomplishment in a long journey. But compared to Lily's life it also seems a small thing. Running a race is nothing like delivering a new body into the world.

Whatever validation of my body's goodness I once sought from a big race, I now find in her—my body echoed and harmonized with Emily's body. My first triathlon was about bragging rights, proving that I could get to the finish line. Since Lily's birth I've viewed Ironman more as a victory lap, a long-distance celebration of this grace-saturated life. To do something significant with the body—to push it far, to move it toward the realization of its potential and fullness—is to glory in it.

Lily is already asleep as I push into the last interval. My legs burn and this feels good, just as it will feel good for them to be sore after the workout, to be real to me once again. I am nearing the final week of training, and these are my last workouts. Emily has started making a packing list and arranged for pet care. Soon we will be on the road to Panama City, Florida, and all my months of training will be tested against the punishing 140.6 miles of the ultimate triathlon. I believe that I can finish. I hope that I can finish. But as the Ironman motto goes, "Anything can happen."

This Is My Body
Fulfilled

Ironman

Panama City is on the west coast of Florida, the Gulf of Mexico side, just down from the collection of Alabama beach towns known as the "Redneck Riviera." The whole place is flat, decorated with pine trees and palms; its only charm is found at its beachfront, looking out over the Gulf. That edge is blunted, though, by high-rise condos and giant T-shirt shops selling neon kitsch that could only appeal to those too hung over to know better. The local economy is a beach economy, but it is even more specialized than that. This isn't a family-friendly beach town like Seaside or Pensacola. This is a place built on the promise of spring break, but the days of blackouts and beer pong, fruity drinks, and Girls Gone Wild are a long way off in this first week of November. The college students are supposed to be studying this time of year, closing in on finals. For this week the town of Panama City shifts gears as it plays host to thousands of athletes from around the world. We started spotting them around Mobile: cars sporting five-thousand-dollar bikes mounted on roof racks and cheesy bumper stickers that say things like "Tri-Harder." Some cars were already branded with the bragging rights of the M-dot: the Ironman logo.

Condos and hotels for miles around are filled with athletes and their cheering squads. The "tri" look is on regular display—lean bodies and clean-shaven, short hair with a visor and sunglasses worn on top. You can see the miles on the bare, shaven legs of both men and women as they stand in the registration lines. Unlike most races, where checking in the day before will do, Ironman requires registrants to come two days before the race's start.

There's plenty for me to do in those two days: drive the course, arrange gear for each segment of the race in special transition bags distributed to athletes, take warm-up rides, check the shifting of every bike gear, and make sure my legs still work by taking a short run. Every step is an opportunity to get negatively amped up on the energy and anxiety of other athletes.

"Avoid the crowds," one wise triathlete counseled me, and I try my best. I have plenty of anxious energy of my own to work out, so I get my gear checked in and my bike racked as early as possible on the day before the race. I want to spend the afternoon loading up on carbs and enjoying the beach.

The last prep-task of the day is to test the water with a warm-up swim. Behind our condo is a buoy just off the beach that athletes are using to practice with, swimming out in groups to circle it and return to the beach. I put my wetsuit on and get in an elevator full of other athletes; we are in no way embarrassed to be gathered together in skin-tight neoprene. Out on the beach, Emily sits with her mom and sister who have come down to help out with the baby. They all watch Lily as she crawls after gulls and then stops, fascinated, to look at shells.

I run into the water like I will on race day and take short dolphin dives until I find myself in water deep enough for swimming. The water is cool, and I am glad for my wetsuit. Between the buoyancy of salt water and the added lift of the wetsuit, the swim feels easy. I do a couple of pickup sprints: *one, two, three, four, five* fast strokes and then rest. I don't want to exhaust my body, but I do want to get my muscles ready on every level. I make the turn around the buoy and catch up with a group of athletes swimming back. I practice swimming my way through the group, just as I will when all two-thousand-plus of us run into the ocean at sunrise the next day.

When I leave the water I feel ready for the next day's swim, but I also feel something else in my body—something out of balance, a cold coming on. When I woke up earlier I had a slight sore throat that I dismissed as having been caused by the air conditioning. But after my swim in the cool of the ocean, my body is clearly telling me I have a virus. By midmorning my nose is running and my lymph nodes are swelling. I go to the Walmart across the street from our condo. Athletes roam the aisles, filling their carts with bagels, bananas, and Powerade. I fill mine with Cold-EEZE, Emergen-C, and every other cold quick-fix I can find. Back at the condo I take my zinc, megadose myself with vitamin C, pray, and let it go.

Sleep doesn't come easily. Emily had insisted that I sleep in the bunk beds outside of the master bedroom in order not to be wakened by Lily's inevitable cries for night nursing. Alone, I lay thinking through the day ahead of me: how the curves of the road will feel when I'm on my bike, what the run will be like. I drift off with these roads in my mind and wake to my alarm at 5 a.m. I drink a fruit smoothie while looking out at the dark of the ocean. I pray in silence, placing my body and my whole self before God. I feel small and yet grand.

As soon as my alarm went off, I was on a schedule designed to get me to the start ready and relaxed. I dress in my triathlon suit, slip shorts and a T-shirt over it, and walk down to the transition area where my bike is waiting. I have a headlamp on; it's still dark outside. Across the parking-lot-turned-transition-area, lights bob as athletes make last-minute bike preparations. I air up my tires to their maximum recommended 120 psi on a set of fast and light aerodynamic wheels my friend Scott loaned me for race day. I stuff food into the bento box strapped on the front of my bike: Bonk Breaker bars and a couple of gels. I shove a water bottle into the holder between my aerobars up front and slide two more bottles—one filled with water, the other with a carbohydrate drink—into the holders behind the bike saddle. With that, I am ready. There's over an hour to kill before I need to be on the beach for the race start.

I stop in at the hotel café and get Emily a vanilla latte, her favorite morning treat. Emily and Lily are just getting up when I arrive back at the condo. I help with Lily as we get ready to go down to the beachfront, surprising even myself with my calm. In my first races I was always filled with anxiety on race morning—an unpleasant person to be around, by Emily's account. But now, with experience, I am able to relax and accept that I am as prepared as I can be.

We all walk down to the beach: Emily with Lily in her stroller; me, carrying the bag that holds my wetsuit, swim cap, and goggles. Athletes and families stream to the water, crowding through to the narrow boardwalk and onto the sand. These friends, spouses, and children —the kids playing in the sand as their fathers and mothers pull on neoprene wetsuits—are already a part of this race; no one gets to an Ironman start line alone. Training for this race is all consuming, so if it isn't done as a pursuit toward health and goodness and a celebration of life, then it isn't worth the sacrifice of hours and energy. The feeling here, at the start of this longest of days, is one of celebration. After all the training, we are all here. In seventeen hours, whether we've made it to the finish line or not, the race will be over.

I pull on my wetsuit and swim cap, kiss Emily and Lily, and pose for a last photo before I say good-bye. In that photo, which I still have,

I am holding Lily, who is nearly a year old. I'm smiling, my body hugged by black rubber, few secrets hidden by my skintight clothes. It is not a body that I am proud of, exactly, but no one needs to be proud of a body. It is a body that I have accepted as *my* body, a gift that will move one day into a fullness of glory come resurrection. In the meantime, I will live into its hope and presence, enjoy its pleasures, and endure its pains. The 140.6 miles ahead of me will include all of that.

I stand at the edge of the Gulf, looking out at that long horizon of the earth's curve. The buoys we'll swim around appear and then disappear in the choppy water. I breathe deeply, feeling my body now caught between the weak feelings brought on by sickness and the strength achieved through training and prayer.

When I woke that morning, my cold had not miraculously disappeared. The soreness in my throat had only increased, but I felt certain I could go on. In fact, the act of that virus replicating its RNA, triggering a cascade of white blood cells in my body, created a sense of spaciousness for me. I wasn't going to meet my goal time, so I could let go of that hope. I was now able to release my body to the distance and the training, to offer my body as a prayer. This was not some "Dear God, give me strength" prayer; it was not even a "Lord, you are so mighty and powerful and full of wonder" kind of prayer. It was a prayer of surrender and release, a prayer that I would push my body to the edges of its possibility in order to experience the deeper embodiment of God.

Bahhh! The horn sounds and I push into the water, diving and wading through the shallows, trying to find a space for my body among the flailing limbs. As I move deeper, the waves high, it's hard to sight the buoys ahead. I swim wide, trying to find some open water and hoping the current pushing me toward the buoy line will offset the effort required to swim the extra distance. There are swimmers everywhere, all two thousand of us starting at once. It seems that with every stroke I am grabbing a foot or feeling a leg. I keep my reach long to make sure

I don't catch a foot in the face. I look up and see a clear path; three rapid strokes and I pass the swimmer ahead of me. Ten minutes in I've found open water, wide of the buoys. I can swim now and think through each moment of my stroke. I keep my head relaxed and down, power through my hips and core, and keep my arms extended. I want to be steady, not fast. By the time I make the turn around the buoy, I am moving into that rhythm that makes any swim a glorious experience.

Suddenly I am at the beach again. I swim into it, keeping a full stroke until my arms brush the sand. This is a two-loop course: 1.2 miles, each loop. I run past a group of volunteers who are handing out water. Grabbing a cup as I pass, I rinse my mouth of salt water and spit it out as I run back into the Gulf. This second loop is easier; the swimmers have spread out with their varied paces. I can keep closer to the buoy line this time, making a straight shot out to the last buoy and then back to the shore. The Velcro at the top of my wetsuit has started to come loose and is rubbing against my neck, creating a painful, raw strawberry that stings in the salt. There is nothing to do. I have to endure it.

I am feeling good now, and as I pass the last turn around the buoys, my body feels full of strength. I am passing lots of swimmers now—those who went out too hard or who weren't as strong as I was in the water. Passing people is a tempting psychological motivator and a dangerous one. I try to stay steady and strong, not to push too hard just so I can pass someone. Then I am up against the sand again. I run out of the water, pull the zipper on the back of my wetsuit, and roll it down to my waist. A team of volunteers stands just beyond the swim exit. I signal to one as I run up and lay down on the boardwalk. He gives a hard tug and my wetsuit pulls off.

I run along the boardwalk, passing under a line of fresh water showers to get the salt off of me. Just beyond the boardwalk swim-to-bike transition, bags are laid out in neat rows by race number. I arranged mine with my beach towel sticking out of the top so I could recognize it quickly. I grab it and continue jogging, barefoot, across the pavement and into the hotel convention center.

Two big rooms are set up for transition: one for women and one for men. I sit down in a long row of chairs and pull my socks, bike shoes, helmet, and sunglasses from the bag. A volunteer comes over and helps me, stuffing my wetsuit into the bag as I put on my shoes. "Good luck," he says as I run off—sliding my helmet over my head, a little hobbled in my bike shoes—toward the big, open garage door that leads to bike transition.

I look for the distinctive tree where I racked my bike, running down the rows until I find it. The bike rack is about half full, meaning I am somewhere near the middle of the pack. I grab the bike and jog beside it, my hand on the seat. There is a big "Bike Out" sign by the exit, clear enough to be seen even by dazed athletes, and I head toward it. The mount line is just beyond the gate. *Click, pedal push, and click.* I am off.

I turn the pedals fast and easy at first, getting my legs warmed up as I race along the hotel exit road. Family members and friends crowd along the roadway; I spot Emily for a moment in the crowd, cheering for me as I pass. At the intersection, I turn left toward the highway, riding past condos and beach bars, T-shirt shops and big box strip malls. I lower my gears and push a little harder, picking up speed on the highway along with a few other riders. We come to a big bay bridge that arches up from the flat landscape, creating the only real hill of the day; it's a hard-breathing climb up, followed by the reward of easy speed down. From there it is *on*—my legs spinning fast and steady, my body bent over my aerobars.

On my wrists I wear the two items that can get me through the ride: my Garmin and Road ID. The Garmin tells me my speed, my heart rate, and the cadence of my pedals. My Road ID, a kind of cyclist's dog tag, carries exactly the message I need to remember: "YOU ARE LOVED" spelled out in all caps, right below my emergency contact information. Emily gave me that bracelet. She gave me the bike that I am riding on, the helmet I am wearing, and the time I needed for training. She knows the power of distance, and she has encouraged me in that knowledge. Hers isn't some selfish hope that her husband will come out of this experience with a better body. She wants to encourage me in a sport that draws me closer to my fullness. *YOU ARE LOVED.* That is the message I hear in the quiet focus of that long ride because Emily shouts it with strength into my life. It is a message Emily heard in her own life, in an almost mystical way—a recurring and profound sense that, with an overcoming and overwhelming love, God and his angels and the communion of saints desire for each person's life to reach its fullness.

Eighty-five, one-forty-eight, two hours and twenty minutes... On my right wrist, my Garmin is keeping the numbers. This isn't in contrast to the message of love; the hard numbers and cold facts of my cadence, heart rate, and time are the tools to help me live into the reality of my body's fullness. It is useless at this point to focus my attention on my speed. If I push myself to maintain a faster speed, I will leap past my aerobic threshold and crash during the marathon. Speed can only be built during training, and the speed I have now is the speed I have to live with. Now I need to keep my pedaling cadence at its most efficient (around ninety revolutions per minute) and keep my heart rate at its best endurance pace (Zone 2). I keep my focus on those numbers, only occasionally clicking my screen over to check my speed and distance.

When I do look at my speed, the numbers aren't good. Around mile fifty I started experiencing cardiac drift; the lines of my speed and heart rate were diverging. I had been staying steadily in Zone 2, a pace that on a flat course would normally allow me to travel at twenty miles per hour over a long distance. But my speed has started to slow. This can be a sign of bad training, but it can also be a sign of illness. My heart is echoing what the rest of my body knows.

I try to eat and drink, but nothing I have on the bike seems palatable. The idea of eating an energy bar makes me feel sick. I try a GU energy gel, and it is overly sweet. Along the course are aid stations staffed by volunteers from community groups and the Boy Scouts; they hand out electrolyte drinks, bottles of water, gummy chews, and GU. It's like a high-speed bazaar—volunteers standing by the roadside holding out their goods and yelling: "GU! Chews! Perform! Water!"

As I approach I throw my water bottles to the side of the road where volunteers are collecting the racers' trash. I grab a bottle of PowerBar Perform, an Ironman-specific electrolyte drink, and a bottle of water from kids who hold them out for an easy and fast exchange. I point at a guy holding out chews and grab one from his hand as I ride by; I pick up a couple more packs of chews from the next volunteers down the line before heading back to the open road.

I'd never trained with the energy chews, but now—over halfway through the race and feeling sick at the thought of my usual race food—I find that I tolerate them the best. I get more at the next aid station, cramming my bento box full. I begin to feel better with the sugars in my body, their short sugar chains split quickly by my metabolism and sent straight into my bloodstream to feed the contracting cells of my muscles.

We pass through farmland, through scrubby pine forests, experiencing as we change roads the wide variety of work quality demonstrated by city, county, and state governments—from smooth to pothole-ridden, to so rough that the course is littered with spare inner tubes and water bottles that have fallen off of bikes.

Over a long race you start to see the same people passing and getting passed by each other, never more than a mile or two apart. I keep seeing two guys in the team uniform of the DC Triathlon Club along the course. Another is a guy I know from back home, the owner of a great Italian place who took up triathlon to lose the weight gain inevitable to his trade. Athletes who sped past early on now reappear as the miles wear on, rejoining those who kept their heart rates and paces steady.

Mile to mile, aid station to aid station, the distance has to be divided up somehow. I keep myself going throughout the monotony by paying attention to the tri-jersey uniforms of different clubs and to the details of the scenery. I watch scrubby pines give way to weedy fields where the poor soil of the Panhandle was overworked by hopeful farmers in the early years. My mind wanders in daydreams while my legs spin in circles; my heart pounds, pushing oxygen to my air-hungry body.

Then the pain comes. My lower back aches after ninety miles spent crouched down in the aero position—my body bent low over my handlebars so I can cut more easily through the wind. I set little goals: *Okay, let's push to the next aid station… Now, the next.* Signs posted along the way bring a smile when the pain is worst: "SEEMED LIKE A GOOD IDEA 365 DAYS AGO" and "CHUCK NORRIS HAS NEVER COMPLETED AN IRONMAN."

Suddenly, out of my daydreams and distractions and pain, I see that I have twenty bike miles to go. About an hour left and then I can run—change the pace and give my back a break. The feelings of illness are subsiding, and as I climb back over the bay bridge into Panama City Beach, I start to push a little harder. I pass cyclists, one after another, moving up the ranks of racers. As I make the turn onto the hotel drive, I lower my gears and spin fast to loosen my legs. Chris, another athlete from Little Rock, calls out my name as I pass through the crowd. Emily and Sally wave at me from the side and I smile back. At the bike dismount line, I clip out my shoes and come to a stop. *Swim: down. Bike: down.* Only a marathon left to run.

I rack my bike and run back into the convention center transition room. Helmet, sweat-smeared sunglasses, bike shoes—into the bag. Running shoes, visor, clean sunglasses—on. Then I'm out the big bay doors and the run-out gate. It feels good to run. I switch my Garmin from bike mode to run mode. My heart rate is steadily in Zone 2. My shoes feel good: Saucony Kinvaras with a low profile and good cushioning. I debated my shoe choice up until the last minute; each pair I own has its advantages and disadvantages. The Kinvaras won because they are a kind of in-between option: minimal, but not too minimal; light and fast, but with enough support in case my running form starts to fall apart in the final miles.

It's hard to gather a crowd along a 112-mile bike course, but on the 13.1 miles of the two-loop run course, this is easier. Near the beginning, along a strip of beachfront houses and small shops, locals are out like wild tailgaters: drinking, offering beer to runners, dressed in wild costumes. Girls in short skirts and wigs dance up to runners passing by. A few spectators are dressed like the Marvel Comics Iron Man; they jump with enthusiasm. Friends and relatives hold up signs for their loved ones, inspirational messages or Bible verses printed in bold lines with an Expo marker. Philippians 4:13 is a favorite: "I can do all things through him who strengthens me."

That verse especially strikes me. It is found toward the end of the book of Philippians, just after Paul has given a whole series of exhortations to the church. In the verse just before it, Paul describes how through Christ he can be at peace whether he is hungry or well fed; he says that he can be joyful in poverty and in plenty. Then comes the message of verse 13: what matters isn't these external things, but the inner strength that comes from our real life source—Christ. I won't finish these final miles through right nutrition or proper pacing, as important as those are. I have to breathe Christ as I breathe the air; I have to surrender to God as the center of my power. "Lord have mercy, Christ have mercy."

The course moves from the beachfront toward the more residential center of the peninsula. We run through suburban neighborhoods. There are houses both big and small; aside from the large number of boats parked in driveways, they look like yards you'd find anywhere else in America. The residents of these neighborhoods are used to the road closures and long streams of runners of the annual race. They help man the aid stations: one every mile throughout the course. It seems like the neighborhoods are competing with each other to show how well they can decorate their stations, how well they can serve the athletes coming through.

It is hot at the beginning of the run. I drink water and Coke at the aid stations. I squeeze ice-water-soaked sponges down my neck and walk for thirty steps before forcing myself to pick up the pace again. With two loops to the course, I occasionally pass other racers from All In Multisport, or "AIM," my triathlon club back home. "Go AIM!" we yell at one another; we exchange the occasional high-five or thumbs-up.

The first quarter of the run ends in a state park at the end of the peninsula. Here the sand dunes and beach grasses of native Florida are preserved in one small stretch of beach. The sun is settling with a golden light over the dunes. My mind goes to beauty—the strong beauty of these bodies all around me, old and young, pushing through the distance. All this is a reflection of the beauty of God, these images of God enduring these miles to see what their bodies can do, how glorious they can be.

The whole idea of Ironman could seem absurd: people spending hours upon hours and thousands of dollars to race some meaningless distance, just for the sake of finishing. Fewer than 5 percent of two thousand athletes will come away with a prize to show for their effort. But those who see pragmatic purpose as a requirement for meaning will often be disappointed. We spend our lives engaged in absurd pursuits and celebrations because the world itself is meaningless when judged by pure pragmatic purpose. Did God create the world for anything more than love and delight? There is no business proposition in that. This is our end and purpose: to love God and to enjoy God in all the vastness of the divine reality. So running a marathon, racing an Ironman, swimming the English Channel, and climbing Mount Everest are all simply celebrations of being human. At their best, such celebrations are also celebrations of the God in whose image we are formed. On any good journey there come dark nights when the waste and excess of our selves, egos, and pride must be cast off. The writer of Hebrews names what must come at the end of any distance: "Let us also lay aside every weight and the sin that clings so closely, and let us run with perseverance the race that is set before us" (12:1).

I am back at the cheering crowds, passing through the tailgating locals who've become a little more drunk with the hours. I spy Emily and Lily as I make the turn that indicates the 13.1-mile mark: halfway through the marathon. I run over and kiss them quickly before circling back out to the second lap. It is getting dark now, and a race organizer gives me a glow necklace to wear, a dim help for the cars that pass close on some parts of the run.

In the darkness my body begins to ache with exhaustion. I can't eat anything; not even the chews work anymore. At an aid station I take a sip of Coke and a sip of water, then toss the rest in the trashcan. Some stations serve warm chicken broth, and I find that goes down the best. "Coke, chicken broth!" I call as I come through the next station. A few sips of each keeping me going, slowly.

I had hoped that during the race I would walk only at the aid stations, but as the miles stretch on, I start walking far beyond the stations' borders. I measure out the distance: *I'm going to run to that light post, and then I can walk...* After a few passes of walking I run to the next target. This is how I continue until I reach the magic number: mile eighteen. At this point I have only a short eight miles left. I've been aiming for this point, saving energy so that I can give the last of myself to those final miles.

Everyone is suffering at this point in the race. I see a man lying on the sidewalk, exhausted, trying to rise and run again. I hear the short bursts of ambulance sirens; athletes who look fit and lean are carried away on stretchers. This is a race that reveals every weakness, every mistake made in nutrition and electrolyte balance. A few miles of the wrong pacing can end the best athlete. *Forward, forward, forward…* A run, a jog, a walk. *Forward* is the consuming thought of my body.

Roger Weldon, the fast athlete who organizes many of our local group rides, says that Ironman is a race that requires each person to reach deep inside for that thing that will get him through the final miles. Before one of his own Ironman races he posted on Facebook: "Goal #1: Finish. 16:59:59 or less. To be a 'Finisher' is to win and represents going into some really dark physical and mental, possibly spiritual, places. No matter what happens, to finish supersedes all other goals." *Forward, forward…* My body trips and moves toward that distant finish line that is beyond my hearing and seeing, but is *there,* somewhere down this road.

I pass through the state park; only one quarter of the distance left. I pass a man in his late sixties or even early seventies; he's barely moving forward but still running, his body contorted by suffering and effort. I hear him praying with each step: "Lord Jesus, Lord Jesus, Lord Jesus." I have been praying my own prayers: "Lord Jesus, have mercy." I've also spent time in the silent awareness that in this body I am in the presence of the divine. Now, my body exhausted by 132 miles and thirteen hours of effort, I pray for the people in my life. I pray for God's blessing on my parents—so full of love and forgiveness—who have always modeled for me the humility to learn and grow in Christ.

I think of Emily, who has brought me here, who has taught me that bodies can pray as much as minds. Emily has returned me to my story as one who is beloved. In that, she has healed my body, reminding me that this skin is no shell but rather a sacrament, a sign of God's love in the world.

I confess to God all those days when I let my self unravel in smoke and ambition. I confess those days when I let my cravings rule my spirit as much as they ruled my body. I confess all the ways I trapped Liz in my hopes and desires. I pray that she too has found her fullness.

In many ways this race has been an attempt to conquer my body, but in these final miles I come to the profound realization that that was never the point. I was surrendering my body. I was letting go of my efforts to make my body fit someone else's definition of shape. I had to let my body be what God gave me and wanted for me. I had to live in hope of the resurrection that will allow me to continue in this body, even with its scars.

The neighborhood streets are dark, the aid stations like beacons in the quiet night. Family members join the runners here and there, encouraging them as they approach the final five miles. *Run just a little more.* I push my body along, but then it slows with the gravity of distance, the miles dragging me down.

"Ragan!" I hear Emily call. "You can do it, babe. You're so close!" She and Sally are suddenly beside me on a dark street. "The finish line is just ahead, just a little more! We'll see you there!"

This is the encouragement I need. I'm ready to give everything left in my body to these last three miles.

I run, not stopping. I'm sloppy and slow, but I'm running. I run through the streets, past the beachside condos where the party is now dying off. I can hear the music at the finish line. I can hear the announcer's loud voice calling out the names of the finishers, each followed by those magic words: "You are an Ironman!"

I pass Alvin's Island, the T-shirt shop that marks the last turn. I run harder; I want to leave everything behind on that road. I run into the long finishing chute plastered with the M-dot logo. People crowd against the finishing gates, waving flags, holding up posters. I give high-fives to the AIM crew cheering me along. Up ahead a big clock counts up the hours, minutes, seconds of the race, and the timing mat marks the end. I make my best effort at a sprint and pass across the mat, its beep signaling the finish.

"Ragan Sutterfield, you are an Ironman!" the words burst from the loudspeakers, and they ring through my body.

I have finished, but I have done more than that. I have discovered that I am beloved—beloved in body, beloved in soul, wrapped in the fullness of love that spills grace from every atom. "Glory to God whose power, working in us, can do infinitely more than we can ask or imagine."[31] Glory to God who gives us glory in our bodies, glory in the lives we live.

I have found my fullness.

This Is My Body,
Now and Forever

The Potomac River looks arctic, iced over and covered with snow. The trail that winds along it is icy in spots, and I have to watch my step, keeping my running form perfect, lest I slip and end my season early. Today I'm running fourteen miles; my weekend long runs will build to twenty before race day. On Easter weekend—the day after we remember the dark murder of God on Good Friday, just before the overcoming love of resurrection Sunday—I will run fifty kilometers, thirty-one miles, through the Blue Ridge Mountains.

This race will be my first significant endurance test since the Ironman. After Ironman there was a need for rest—time to simply be a father and husband without also trying to work in so much training in the spare time I didn't have. I trained for shorter triathlons, and I tried to work up the motivation to sign up for some longer runs. But though my body was ready, my mind and spirit weren't.

In the meantime I began to feel a different kind of call on my body. My hunger grew for the physical connection with God that finds fulfillment in the kneeling and standing of *The Book of Common Prayer,* the bread and wine of Eucharist. I felt that perhaps I was being called to be a priest. I wanted to be as close as possible to the bread and the wine; I wanted to help others find that connection to the body of God that would lead to their own incarnation, their own discovery that God created and loves their bodies.

I asked others to join with me in listening to what God was saying about this; we spent nearly a year in focused discernment during which we prayed together, and I answered many questions from wise members of my church. In the end what we all heard together was that this was a "Yes" in my life. Next came conversations with my bishop, seminary applications, scholarship applications, and a move to Virginia. Now my days are filled with Christology and Church History, Greek participles and New Testament exegesis. They are also marked by a meal that we all are called to, that my classmates and I are learning to serve.

Every weekday at seminary we gather to eat the bread and drink the wine. We remember that night when Jesus gathered his disciples around the Last Supper and took a loaf and broke it, poured a cup and offered it. "In the beginning was the Word" reads the gospel of John (1:1). This word was the *logos,* the logic of all reality, the organizing meaning of the world. But to save the world, to bring it back to the divine, God didn't come as a ghostly mind offering spiritual insight. God came as flesh: a body that was broken and shared.

It was the eating of that flesh—not the reading of Scriptures, not preaching, not any other ornate or important religious trapping—that was the central act of the early church. The church became the church around the strange act of eating the sign of an embodied God and of drinking wine that reminded them that this God bled. In eating the bread and drinking the wine, they could imagine their flesh and their blood becoming fused with and fueled by Christ.

The Eucharist is an act that brings one body into a community of bodies. In the Anglican tradition of which I am a part, the priest is not allowed to prepare communion if no one is gathered to receive it. The Eucharist is only meaningful in the context of a community. It is preparation for a banquet.

Throughout the Scriptures, the recurring image of a feast represents a time when all things will be set right: a meal at which death and suffering will be no more, and a life of celebration will be ours to enjoy for eternity.

> On this mountain the LORD of hosts will make for all
>   peoples
> a feast of rich food, a feast of well-aged wines,
> of rich food filled with marrow, of well-aged wines
>   strained clear.
> And he will destroy on this mountain the shroud that
>   is cast over all peoples,
> the sheet that is spread over all nations; he will swallow
>   up death forever. (Isaiah 25:6–8)

This meal is one to which all of creation is invited, no longer alienated from each other through violence, all embraced in the reality of shalom, health, peace, and well-being. I imagine that at this feast there will be dancing and that, as at any good dance, a host of bodies will move to the music—music as we've never heard. I imagine God will be the bandleader of the music, moving along with the rhythm of the bodies.

In the Christian view, God is a community, a Trinity of being. This is an idea that's hard to grasp, one long wrestled with by theologians. Within this idea exists the possibility that love requires relationship. A God who is a single being, without anyone with whom to have a relationship, could never be named Love. But a God who is a family—Father, Son, and Holy Spirit—is a God who embodies Love itself. Within God's own self there is a relationship between the persons of the Trinity, and God is ready to bring us into that relationship as well. In attempts throughout the ages to represent this reality, Christians have returned again and again to the image of a dance: the three members of the Trinity, distinct but together, moving in response to one another and to their shared divine rhythm. When we hear that same beat and move our bodies to it, we enter into that divine life ourselves.

I have always been a hesitant dancer, not because I disliked the movements but because my body always felt awkward and exposed. But as I surrender my body to the divine rhythm, as I join the communion of saints in the banquet of Love and consciously let go of my ego, how can I not now join the dance?

On the night Emily and I were married, Father Ed said in the ceremony that our purpose was to "make love visible." In the community of love that is our marriage, we are to reflect God's community of Love; we are to be love-with-flesh. That night of our wedding, after the liturgy, we gathered upstairs at the church with friends for dinner and dancing. The band was a wild mix of accordions and violins, drums and tambourines—a modern Gypsy band. I took Emily's hand and we stepped to the dance floor. My body moved with her body; the bodies of our friends and families moved around us, dancing and clapping in joy. In Emily's eyes, I saw her love reflecting Christ's love, a smiling icon.

In that moment I was aware of my body in skin and muscle, bone and blood—imperfect and wonderful. I was unashamed. I pulled Emily more tightly against me, and we moved to the wild beats. This is my body, her body, our bodies saturated in joy. In sickness and health, in life and someday in death, we will dance in this gift of skin.

We are practicing for forever.

Acknowledgments

I was in the shower of the Downtown Athletic Club, rinsing off after a hard afternoon training session, when I first conceived of this book. Before my workout I'd had a conversation with my friend Fred Bahnson about writing books. "For good narrative nonfiction, you've got to have a story worth telling," Fred had said, and I'd been repeating that to myself through the workout. Lathered with soap, washing the sweat from my skin, I realized that I had a story about my body that reached all the way back to childhood. *This is my body,* I thought. *I want to write a book about it.* It was many months later that the book began to take shape, and it has been two years now since I started my work on it. There are many people to thank for bringing this book about, more than I can likely remember, but I want to name a few.

I owe deep gratitude to Fred Bahnson. He not only encouraged me from the beginning, he gave me the gift of an introduction to his agent and kept helping me with edits and encouragement through the completion of the entire manuscript. His advice and comments on the text have been invaluable.

This book wouldn't have gone far without Wendy Sherman, my agent. She embraced this project from the first query and guided me expertly through the world of book proposals and contracts. Most importantly, she took the time to help me shape the story, reminding me to help readers "feel the sweat" of my journey.

Ken Petersen at Convergent was quick to embrace the proposal, seeing from the start the value of my story as a means of exploring the troubled relationship between body and soul. His comments on the manuscript brought the book deeper clarity and focus.

Shari MacDonald Strong was my primary editor at Convergent. Her incredible eye for detail and careful reading have made this a far better and more beautiful book than when I first turned the manuscript over to her. She is a reader's advocate, always questioning any place where I was unclear, helping me explain the difficult material covered in these pages.

Much of this book was written while I was in school at Virginia Theological Seminary. I must thank Joyce Mercer, who led me there through an independent study on the theology of the body. Also thanks are due to Mitzi Budde at the Bishop Payne Library, who kindly provided me with a private carrel where I was able to write and edit this book to its completion.

My body, my life, and my faith would not have been possible without my parents, Ken and Jan Sutterfield. They encouraged me, prayed for me, and loved me through the difficult journeys I write about in this book, even when I was too ashamed to share with them all of what I was going through. Their life of faith and deep humility in following the ways of Jesus were like beacons for me in the darkness and continue to guide me.

Finally, I must thank Emily, to whom this book is dedicated. She loved my body and showed me how to love it too. But more than that, she showed me how to bring the life of my body into the life of my soul. She was the first editor of this book, reading every page, catching errors, and helping me make my ideas clearer. Just as critically, she helped me make the time to write it, daring to let me quit my job for a time, and then helping me sneak off in the early hours to keep writing once I was in school. This book is hers as much as it is mine. With her I offer thanks to our daughter, Lillian, whose smile always brings us joy and who helped me take essential play breaks.

Notes

1. Marla Paul, "Religious Young Adults Become Obese by Middle Age," Northwestern University website, March 23, 2011, www .northwestern.edu/newscenter/stories/2011/03/religious-young -adults-obese.html.

2. Christopher Lasch, *The Revolt of the Elites and the Betrayal of Democracy* (New York: Norton, 1995), 28.

3. *Walden and Other Writings of Henry David Thoreau,* ed. Brooks Atkinson, Modern Library Edition (New York: Random House, 1992), 204.

4. Dallas Willard, interview by Lyle SmithGraybeal, "A Conversation with Dallas Willard about Renovation of the Heart," *Renovaré Perspectives* 12, no. 4 (October 2002): 3–5, http://blog.renovare .org/wp-content/uploads/2012/11/perspective_12_4.pdf.

5. "Gregory of Nyssa (c.335–c.395 C.E.)," Internet Encyclopedia of Philosophy, www.iep.utm.edu/gregoryn/.

6. Dominique Luongo and Sylvia Marks, "Study Suggests Eating Disorders More Common Than Thought Among Teen Males," *The Harvard Crimson,* November 20, 2013, www.thecrimson .com/article/2013/11/20/new-study-published-on-eating -disorders. And Paul W. Gallant, "Males' Body Image and Eating Disorders: An Increasing Concern," National Eating Disorder Information Centre website, http://nedic.ca/males-body-image -and-eating-disorders-increasing-concern.

7. "Gary Snyder and Wendell Berry in conversation with Jack Shoemaker." (Recorded Wednesday, November 10, 1999, Santa Fe, NM.)

8. Rob Bell, *Sex God* (Grand Rapids, MI: Zondervan, 2007), 40.

9. "Central Governor with Tim Noakes," interview by Ben Greenfield, *Ben Greenfield Fitness Podcast* no. 138.

10. Walt Whitman, "I Sing the Body Electric," www .poetryfoundation.org/poem/174740.

11. *The Apology, Phaedo and Crito by Plato,* ed. Charles W. Eliot, The Five Foot Shelf of Classics, vol. 2 (New York: Cosimo Classics, 2010), 112.

12. Augustine, "Sermon 240" in *Sermons on the Liturgical Seasons,* trans. Mary Sarah Muldowney, R.S.M., The Fathers of the Church, vol. 38 (Washington DC: Catholic University of America Press, 2008), 262.

13. Martin Luther, *Works,* ed. Robert H. Fischer, Word and Sacrament III, vol. 37 (Philadelphia: Fortress, 1986), 72.

14. Paul Althaus, *The Theology of Martin Luther* (Philadelphia: Fortress, 1966), 376.

15. Brad Leithauser, "Why We Should Memorize," *The New Yorker* online (January 25, 2013), www.newyorker.com/books/page-turner/why-we-should-memorize.

16. Jack Kerouac, *On the Road* (1957; repr., New York: Penguin, 1999), 5.

17. Wendell Berry, "The Body and the Earth" in *The Unsettling of America: Culture and Agriculture* (San Francisco: Sierra Club, 1977), 103.

18. Berry, *The Unsettling of America,* 103.

19. Berry, *The Unsettling of America,* 104.

20. *Chariots of Fire,* directed by Hugh Hudson, Twentieth Century Fox, 1981.

21. Thomas Merton, *New Seeds of Contemplation* (2003; repr., New York: New Directions, 2007), 88.

22. Lawrence Cunningham, *Thomas Merton and the Monastic Vision* (Grand Rapids, MI: Wm. B. Eerdmans, 1999), 1.

23. Wendell Berry, *This Day: Collected and New Sabbath Poems* (Berkeley, CA: Counterpoint, 2014), 150.

24. Athanasius, *The Life of Antony and the Letter to Marcellinus,* ed. Robert C. Gregg (Mahwah, NJ: Paulist Press, 1980), 42.

25. Susanne Gillmayr-Bucher, "Body Images in the Psalms," *Journal for the Study of the Old Testament* 28 (June 2004): 325.

26. E. Stanley Jones, *Victory Through Surrender* (Nashville: Abingdon, 1966), 33, 34, 124.

27. Dallas Willard, *The Spirit of the Disciplines* (1990; repr., New York: Harper One, 1999), 101 (italics in original).

28. Augustine, *The City of God Against the Pagans,* Cambridge Texts in the History of Political Thought, ed. R. W. Dyson (Cambridge, UK: The Press Syndicate of the University of Cambridge, 1998), 1150.

29. G. K. Chesterton, *Twelve Types* (London: AMS Press, 1906), 171.

30. Athanasius, *On the Incarnation,* "Refutation of the Gentiles," chapter 8, Christian Classics Ethereal Library, www.ccel.org/ccel/athanasius/incarnation.ix.html.

31. Ephesians 3:20, *The Book of Common Prayer,* 102.

233.5 SUTTERFIELD

Sutterfield, Ragan.
This is my body

R4001566693

SEAST

SOUTHEAST
Atlanta-Fulton Public Library